Books, Children and Men

BOOKS

CHILDREN

AND MEN

by PAUL HAZARD
Member of the French Academy

Translated by Marguerite Mitchell

Fifth edition
with an introduction by Sheila A. Egoff

THE HORN BOOK, INCORPORATED · BOSTON

Printed in the United States of America

Library of Congress Cataloging in Publication Data

Hazard, Paul, 1878-1944.
    Books, children and men.
    Translation of: Les livres, les enfants et les hommes.
    Bibliography: p.
    Includes index.

1. Children's literature — History and criticism. 2. Children —
Books and reading.   I. Title.

PN1009.A1H33   1983   809'.89282   82-25851

ISBN 0-87675-059-5

PREFACE TO THE
FIFTH EDITION

"IT is Paul Hazard's point of view which has endeared his book to us so durably. Always he writes about children's books as a part of the whole field of literature and art, not as a special field unworthy of the serious attention of critics," wrote Bertha Mahony Miller, in her preface to the first edition of *Books, Children and Men* in 1944. "Because of the 'scholar's holiday' atmosphere of the book, and its critical power, and because it is a limited survey or 'some thoughts concerning' books, children and men, rather than an exhaustive history, this book will, we believe, influence future writing for children in America."

Paul Hazard's views, scholarly but expressed "with gaiety and gusto" as Mrs. Miller noted, continue to be a source of inspiration for all who create and appreciate books for children and who carry on, again in turbulent times, with bringing books and children together.

For this fifth edition, Professor Sheila A. Egoff, of the School of Librarianship at the University of British Columbia in Vancouver, has written an introduction. Information about Paul Hazard and about the translation of the book, written by Marguerite Mitchell, and reminiscences about Paul Hazard by his colleague in the French Department of Columbia University, Dr. Horatio Smith, have been retained in an appendix. An index has been added.

CONTENTS

V THE SOUL OF MAN

APPENDIX

INTRODUCTION

SINCE the first publication in America of *Books, Children and Men* in 1944, there has been a rising flood of books about children's literature published in the English-speaking world. Why then a fifth edition of a book written by a Frenchman over fifty years ago, a publication which has never been revised, and which hardly mentions a book that originated after the nineteenth century? The answer, I think, lies in C. S. Lewis's famous aphorism: "All that is not eternal is eternally out of date." *Books, Children and Men* cannot be outdated: it shines forth like a beacon, a lighthouse in stormy waters. In the midst of conflicting theories about what today's children should or should not read, Paul Hazard speaks of the fundamental aspects of literature and childhood. His central theme is that the essential power of literature is to give wings to the imagination; and that the essence of childhood is to recognize and desire that freedom. The fusing of the two results in the humanistic view of society and the education of the heart.

If this sounds too lofty and idealistic for our times, it should be remembered that Paul Hazard wrote what he himself considered a crucial work during the troubled 1930's, when the stability of Europe was already being threatened. This became a period when not only the survival of literature but the survival of childhood itself was in peril. Yet he gave the world a testament of his unfaltering faith in children, literature, and society at large.

Written at a time that demanded courage and constancy, *Books, Children and Men* serves as a directional light that continues to illuminate the path of children's literature today. While many modern books on children's literature offer excellent surveys, reading guidance, or critical insights, Hazard's work remains a Pierian spring to which one returns for refreshment and renewal. His inspiration encourages one to look beyond the contemporary fragmentation of children's literature into genres or styles or age levels. His vision is vast and comprehensive; it is a vision of integration. Even when he salutes the national contributions of England, France, Germany or the United States, he does so in the spirit of "the republic of childhood' [in which] "each nation gives and each nation receives."

It is also his genius to make such lofty analysis concrete. He is a portraitist rather than a landscape painter; he gives children's literature its human face. How "Puss in Boots," "Cinderella," Gerda of Andersen's "The Snow Queen," "Robinson Crusoe," "Gulliver" leap from his pages and demand attention as companions of childhood!

With the same power with which he celebrates children's allies, he attacks their enemies. How he defends children against their "oppressors" — those who would destroy imagination! The didactic and pragmatic Berquins, Mrs. Trimmers and Thomas Days of children's literature are neatly and firmly put in their isolated place. Not that Paul Hazard despises information. "I like," he says, "books of knowledge . . . when they have tact and moderation; when, instead of pouring out so much material on a child's soul that it is crushed, they plant in it a seed that will develop from the inside."

Paul Hazard not only values the soul of childhood, he also cherishes children as individuals able to appreciate quality of thought and authenticity of emotion, whether they are exposed to them in life or in literature. He praises such books as those that provide an intuitive way of knowledge, an awakening of sensibility, and a profound morality. But, he says, "to misshape young souls, to profit by a certain facility that one may possess to add to the number of indigestible and sham books, to give oneself too easily the airs of a moralist and scholar, to cheat in quality — that is what I call oppressing children."

Gleams of prescience, intimations of a future that has become our present, balance this fundamental perspective on childhood and its literature. Will childhood dwindle to a rare species, vanish entirely, exchange roles with adulthood? He senses this possibility and feels the world would be impoverished by it.

It is possible that one may disagree with Paul Hazard's deep-rooted idealism, but no lover of literature could be unaffected by his style. He writes with the rich knowledge of a scholar, the skill of a litterateur, and with the qualities that he himself attributes to the folktale — "humor, charm, freshness and a dash of poetry."

Books, Children and Men now comes to us in a new edition. For all concerned with children and their books, it is a raising of our consciousness, a life preserver for our spirit, and it comes none too soon.

SHEILA A. EGOFF

University of British Columbia
Vancouver, Canada
October 12, 1982

I

MEN HAVE ALWAYS OPPRESSED

CHILDREN

Give Us Wings!

CHILDREN and grownups belong to different worlds. Time, which deals so ruthlessly with the body, is only too often just as pitiless with the soul. Adults are rarely free; they are prisoners of themselves. Even when they play it is self-consciously and for a reason. They play in order to relax, to forget, to keep from thinking of the brief time that is still left to them. They seldom play for the sheer joy of playing.

How far removed is the world of childhood! Its inhabitants seem of another species. Tireless, full of the exuberance of life, from morning to night they run, shout, quarrel, make up and fall asleep only to begin again next day at sunrise. Their awkward young bodies are already imperious. Children are rich with all they do not own, rich with the potential wonders of their universe. Making believe is not only one of their earliest pleasures, it is their vital spark, the token of their liberty. Reason does not curb them, for they have not yet learned its restraints. Happy beings, they live in the clouds, playing light-heartedly without a care.

But imagination cannot keep alive by itself, and the spirit, too, requires food, since we do not live by bread alone. So children turn to those who give them home, clothes, love, everything they need; to the friendly powers that comfort and protect them in this strange universe — this drama in which, for children, wolves and bogies lurk at every dark corner. They beg for pictures and stories which they immediately alter or destroy, or turn into something which suits their own fancy better. And they must have plenty of them, an abundance, for they are hard to satisfy. We have no sooner finished telling a tale than they cry: " Begin all over again! " No sooner have they learned to read, than they expect wonders of those little black letters that come to life before their eyes. These magic books are such a joy! They see a whole new world opening before them, a world in which they will still be playing, but at far vaster games. Now they need no longer beg their mother to rack her brains, tease her to tell over and over again those stories that she loved when she was a little girl, just as she in turn had begged her own mother, long ago. How wonderful it will be to turn over the pages for themselves, to discover even better and more wonderful stories! And here begins the history of a long misunderstanding.

Except for a few privileged persons, a few madmen, a few poets who, by some gift from Heaven, have understood the language of children as the fairies understand that of birds, adults failed for a long time to grant their prayers. Entirely pleased with themselves, they offered the child books that represented themselves, with all their attributes thrown in, their practical sense, their science, their hypocrisy and their ankylosis. They offered him books that oozed boredom, that were likely to make him detest wisdom forever; silly books and empty books, pedantic books and heavy books; books that paralyzed the spontaneous forces of his soul; absurd books by tens and by hundreds, falling like hail on the springtime. The sooner they stifled a young heart, the sooner they effaced from a young spirit the sense of freedom and pleasure in play; the sooner they imposed limits, rules and constraints, the more men were pleased with themselves for having raised childhood without delay to their own state of supreme perfection.

Yesterday was even more oppressive than today. Yesterday men were more cramped by their prejudices. Surer of possessing the truth without the shadow of a doubt, they were more stern and domineering. Not that they acted from unkindness, but rather from stupidity, from a false perspective, a lack of suppleness; from the idea of a superior wisdom that knows all of life's secrets and would believe itself disgraced if it learned anything from childhood. For it is due to their own sad state that grownups have never understood children completely, and that the history of their relations with those they love contains misunderstanding, discordant rhythms, good intentions that seldom achieve their purpose. They do not act from unkindness, but the fact remains that, hearing childhood ask for their help, grownups refuse to give it what it needs, and offer it instead what it

3

detests. As a substitute for stories that bring sunshine, they offer it some useful bit of massive and indigestible knowledge, some good bit of authoritative ethics to be applied externally without any internal consent.

We can hear those voices in turn, children and men, talking together without understanding each other:

"Give us books," say the children; " give us wings. You who are powerful and strong, help us to escape into the faraway. Build us azure palaces in the midst of enchanted gardens. Show us fairies strolling about in the moonlight. We are willing to learn everything that we are taught at school, but, please, let us keep our dreams."

"Our children know how to read and are growing up," say the adults; " they are asking us for books. We'd better take advantage of their wishes and their curiosity. Let's pretend to build the castles they are so crazy about, but build them with our own superior wisdom. We'll have a few classrooms concealed in their palaces, and we'll plant vegetables in their gardens, which they will take for flowers. We'll have reason and order and wisdom and natural history and physics and chemistry turn up by chance along the winding paths. While we seem to be telling them familiar nursery tales, they will really be listening to stories full of knowledge. They are so innocent they will never notice, and while they think they are having fun, they will actually be learning from morning to night."

Grownups want to suppress that happy interval of years in which we live without dragging the weight of life about with us, rich years in which our being is

4

not only shaping itself, but receiving in advance its best share of happiness. They destroy those child landscapes that giants cover with great strides, where dwarfs crouch under the roots of the trees; those landscapes where the river talks with the fields that it bathes, and where the skies open up to let a flock of fairies through. They want to exploit the forests, capture the springs, and, without losing a second, build factories. They even resort to trickery. They announce that they are going to take the child for a walk through the fields, but it is really to teach him surveying. They say they are going to take him to Uncle Tom's where he will find a tea party and friends of his own age. It turns out that Uncle Tom is fond of physics and treacherously begins a course of lectures on electricity or on the laws of gravitation. Not only do they rob imagination of its rightful place and declare war on dreams, but they want the youngsters to repeat in all faith: " I am learning, but without seeming to do so; I give up my lovely play hours to study, but I am not even conscious of it. They give me the opposite of what I ask for, but if anyone suspects it, it is not I; I am yawning, therefore I am thrilled; and I am bored, so I am enjoying myself."

Perrault's Fairy Tales

In museums we see portraits painted by the old masters of little girls dressed in the fashion of their day. How they must have suffered in those narrow slippers and heavy velvet skirts, with waist imprisoned in a corset, ribbons hugging the neck, plumed hat crushing the head, to say nothing of necklaces and rings, bracelets and brooches! We long to free them, to give them soft and dainty frocks suitable to young bodies. We long, too, to free those little imitation men who are strapped up rigidly in boots and armor and wear, in spite of their heroic pose, such a ridiculous and unhappy air. If, for centuries, grownups did not even think of giving children appropriate clothes, how would it ever have occurred to them to provide children with suitable books?

We will pass over the era of manuscripts that were not meant to be playthings; and over the era in which reading was the privilege of scholars; but when printing came along and, during the Renaissance, everyone was freed, what did the grownups do then for children? Practically nothing. They were satisfied to let a few crumbs — books of piety, of manners — fall from the upper tables; and if the children were not pleased, so much the worse, for they had no voice in the matter. Let them beg for tales from their nurses, from the servants, the kitchen folk, the common people. Printed tales were for grownups, not for children. Printing was not invented for babes; or if it was, to a certain extent, it undertook only to repeat the Bible to them, the Ten Commandments or the ABC. If they were absolutely determined to be amused, let them turn to the Latin authors — to Ovid, where they would at least find metamorphoses, to Virgil, or to Statius. They reasoned peremptorily that the Latin authors must necessarily delight the little ones since they delighted grownups.

At what moment did the thought first occur to someone that children might wish for other reading than school work, for other books than catechisms or grammars? What revolutionary first became aware of the child's existence and dared to sanction it? What

6

perspicacious observer noticed children? What benefactor procured for them the joy, multiplied to infinity, of owning a book at last that was truly theirs?

That startling event happened in France; not without long preparation, not without infinite trouble. It needed whole centuries to weave and reweave, in the background, the web of which the stories were made. It needed the century of Louis XIV, weary of the heroic, weary even of classicism, to encourage a new interest in the cult of the fabulous, for tales to invade the drawing room and become the fashionable rage. It needed women (always more impassioned) to have them printed, after having related them to their men- and women-friends: Madame d'Aulnoy, Mademoiselle L'Héritier, Mademoiselle Bernard. It needed, in between times, a meddlesome Academician who had a taste for paradox and scandal, and who took it into his head to put into verse " The Patient Griselda," " Foolish Wishes," and " The Ass's Skin."[1] Not, however, without arousing again the anger of Boileau, who spoke scornfully of " The Ass's Skin " and of " The Woman with a Sausage on Her Nose," put into verse by a Monsieur Perrault of the French Academy. It needed Charles Perrault, who went from verse to prose, uncertain, a little bit ashamed, and hiding under cover of his son's name, P. Darmancour. For an Academician may compose burlesque poems if he wants to; he can prefer the Moderns to the Ancients and loose the tempest at will, but the unheard-of thing is that he should dare to publish tales for children.

He did dare, however, when in 1697 he handed to Barbin his *Histoires ou Contes du temps passé, avec*

[1] First published in *Recueil de pièces curieuses et nouvelles, tant en prose qu'en vers.* 1696-1697.

des moralités. Then Mother Goose[1] came out of the sheds and barns and strutted about Paris; then and for the first time, French children, and later all the children in the world, had a book after their own heart, a book so lovely and so fresh that they were never willing to give it up. Never will they forget the " Little Red Riding Hood " whom the wolf devoured so wickedly. Never will they forget " Hop o' My Thumb " and the emotions that stirred their soul so deeply. Pity, when the poor woodcutters have worked in vain, they cannot feed their children and they are obliged to abandon them. Fear, when the poor children are lost in the forest — they have nothing to eat, night comes, and the wind wails through the branches. Anguish and hope alternate. They happen to take refuge in an Ogre's house, and the Ogre's wife wants to save them. The hungry Ogre smells young flesh and wants to cut their throats and the clever Hop o' My Thumb manages so well that the Ogre is fooled into cutting the throats of his own children. Terror, when the Ogre sharpens his great knife, puts on his seven-league boots, rushes forth, leaps over rivers and woods, and comes roaring to the cave where the fugitives are resting. Joy! How happy the mother is to find her little ones again, how she hugs them, and how they return her kisses! Later in life these readers of "Hop o' My Thumb" will see many dramas. They will see some that happen on the stage and some that happen in real life; but never, as long as they live, will they see any that will make their hearts beat more violently. And when, later on by chance, they look

[1] The frontispiece of this edition showed an old woman spinning and telling a tale to three children, and bore the inscription *Contes de ma mère l'Oie* — Tales of Mother Goose.

8

upon the most beautiful places in the world, they will never find one more thrilling than that stretch of green meadow under the golden sun where Anne, my sister Anne, gazing despairingly towards the horizon, sees at last the two brothers arriving at full gallop to free their sister; those two intrepid brothers, one a musketeer, and the other a dragoon; one Salvation, and the other, Life.

And what laughter! How sly and comical that Puss in Boots is, who boasts so much about his master's fortune that he finally succeeds in having him marry the King's daughter! He profits by every circumstance — a bath, a stroll, or a call. The children will never forget him running through the countryside on his little booted paws, threatening to have the peasants beheaded if they refuse to say that the vineyards and wheat and hayfields belong to the Marquis of Carabas, his lord. They will never forget him, entering fearlessly into the Ogre's palace, and asking him to change himself into a mouse. The Ogre obeys — vain, silly thing that he is. Quick as a wink, Puss in Boots jumps on him and gobbles him up alive. We shall laugh over that the rest of our lives.

Perrault is as fresh as the dawn. We never reach the end of his accomplishments. He is full of mischief, humor and charming dexterity. He never seems to be achieving a *tour de force,* lifting a weight, looking for applause, but he seems to be having more fun than anyone, relating these prodigious stories entirely for his own pleasure. From time to time he appears, says a word, starts up a dialogue, then quickly withdraws, realizing that of all faults indiscretion is the clumsiest. These characters should act by themselves, he is only there to do their will, to record their conversation. And his clear language! And his simplicity! "The one quality we can never praise enough," as Sainte-Beuve said, the one that touches all souls.

Fairies in Retreat

Starting off with a masterpiece was too good to be true. But the summer is soon over; all holidays must come to an end. Somehow, before long, fairies seemed to become enemies. They had reigned only for a brief moment, taking advantage of an interval of recreation between a majestic century that was losing its authority and a critical century that had not yet found its own. Now intellect, reason, were all the fashion. How could the fairies hold out against these powers that seemed so intolerant? Knowledge was to clarify the whole universe, and the fairies had no end of trouble finding retreats where they could hide and await better times. The crazy idea that a great author could write for children was speedily dismissed to make way for the idea that we must use pleasure for instruction. Not that the idea was so bad, but instruction took upon itself to suppress pleasure entirely. Children were given medicine with just a drop of honey in it.

In 1757 appeared an epoch-making book, *Magasin des Enfants,* by Madame Leprince de Beaumont. Translated its full title was *The Children's Magazine, or Conversation of a Wise Governess with her most distinguished pupils, in which young people are made to think, speak and act according to the talent, temperament and inclinations of each one. The faults of their age are set forth, a way is shown to correct them; as much attention is paid to molding the heart as to guid-*

ing the spirit. Included is a summary of Sacred History, of Fable, of Geography, etc., the whole filled with useful reflections and moral tales to entertain them pleasantly and written in a simple style suitable to the tenderness of their souls, by Madame Leprince de Beaumont.

Madame Leprince de Beaumont called herself a "Wise Governess." Disappointed in matrimony, she switched to education, crossed the Channel and became a teacher in England. *Magasin des Enfants* was one of seventy volumes that came from her indefatigable pen. In these books imagination and sensibility are no longer considered of value in themselves, but as the means which a wise governess employs to make knowledge more palatable. Now arrives that dreadful moment when it will be decreed that children have not a minute to lose, not a single one, and that even during their play they must endeavor to become little old men as quickly as possible.

To tell the truth, Madame de Beaumont was a trifle uncertain about all this, because she was also fond of poetry and interested in people. "Those who write tales are not necessarily falsifiers," she said, seeking extenuating circumstances for them, "since they are not trying to deceive anyone." She is unconsciously excusing herself, for she told some charming tales; and because she wrote "Beauty and the Beast" she can be forgiven many other things. Let us never forget that lovely, subtle story of bygone days. Do you remember how Beauty was persecuted by her jealous sisters, because she was not only the prettiest, but the most virtuous in the whole world? Do you remember the loving and tender Beast, who was so ill-shapen that he despaired of meeting a woman who would return his love? When Beauty arrived at the Beast's palace she was more pampered than a queen. Her wishes were granted even before they were expressed. She was served delicious food in gold dishes. She was lulled by divine music. In the garden the roses had scarcely less perfume than those in Paradise. But every time that the Beast presented himself before Beauty, with the hope that his attentions would prove worthy of her love, Beauty was shocked by his appearance and could offer him only her friendship. So far did it go that the monster, stretched on the sward, would have died of despair had not love finally been born, out of pity. And as soon as her love was born, his ugliness disappeared.

" No, my dear Beast, you shall not die," Beauty said to him; " you shall live to become my husband. From this very moment I give you my hand and I swear to you that I shall be only yours. Alas! I thought I felt only friendship for you, but the pain I suffer makes me realize that I could not live without you." Hardly had Beauty pronounced these words, than she saw the palace shining with lights, fireworks; there was music and everything that suggested a festival. But all these splendors could not hold her attention. She turned again to her dear Beast whose peril had made her shudder. To her surprise the Beast had disappeared and she now saw at her feet a Prince handsomer than love, who thanked her for having broken the spell.

When anyone writes like that does she not deserve great indulgence as well as admiration?

But meanwhile, the " Wise Governess " was growing affected. Tales, she said, should inculcate the spirit of geometry in children. This was a phrase that she repeated proudly — " the spirit of geometry "; and also, the " empire of reason." " Everything that is told to children, or written for them, everything placed before their eyes must be filled with this spirit, and be brought about by a skilful teacher "— or by a Wise Governess. We can almost hear her solemn voice, and see her, transforming the fairies' wand into a ruler. She named the characters of her dialogues so no one could mistake their meaning — Mademoiselle Goodness, Governess to Lady Sensible; Lady Sensible, twelve years old; Lady Witty, twelve years old; Lady Trinket, seven years old; Lady Tempest, thirteen years old — and she gave them an amusing and natural air, like this:

Lady Witty:
Just what are the Low Countries?

Mademoiselle Goodness:
That stretch of country which is between the North Sea, France and Germany; called thus because they are situated towards the sea and because the land is flat in most sections and of slight elevation elsewhere. They differentiate them into Northern Low Countries or Protestant, and Southern Low Countries, or Catholic.

That is the way to entertain children, if only one knows how to go about it. She cut up history and mythology into little pies -- cleverly, as she thought. She changed even the Bible stories into a strange mixture which she served portion by portion. The pleasure part grew less and less, to the point of disappearing; the pedagogical grew more and more until it invaded everything. The more pedantic she became, the more pleased she was with herself; her pleasure finally knew no bounds.

In truth, this is a melancholy story we are telling. Perrault, Madame d'Aulnoy and the others were springtime; the flowers were about to bloom. Then we see the blossoms wither, the lovely promised garden abandoned all too soon.

Madame de Genlis

About the middle of the eighteenth century the great voice of Rousseau was heard throughout Europe, that voice which disturbed everybody's conscience and reopened all the questions in art, politics and love. As Rousseau aimed to regenerate mankind he found it necessary to begin at the base and deal with education. Not that he was at all interested in books for children, *Robinson Crusoe* being the only one he allowed his Emile to read, but he intended to stand out for the rights of the spontaneous and natural as opposed to those of the mechanical and artificial; and that is what we call a revolution.

After the writers had listened carefully to Rousseau, had absorbed his maxims and had turned with fresh interest towards their child public, they proceeded to do exactly the opposite of what he wanted them to do. The moment they took up their pens they disregarded this primitive, spontaneous master whom they had praised so highly. They employed nothing but artifice, and while pretending to liberate the child's soul, they oppressed it still further. Those very pedagogues who boasted that they worked only in the open air, who talked constantly about the benefits of sunshine, rain and even wind, put their plants in hothouses, forced them, pruned them, directed their growth scientifically. They were even more tyrannical than Lenôtre, who at least did not boast of being more natural than nature.

14

Perhaps the reason for all this was that each time their master, Rousseau, took three bold steps forward, he then took three timid steps back, alternating between revolutionary and reactionary. Regardless of the fact that he had extolled an education without constraint, he placed the pupil under a teacher who supervised everything he did, and who, if he found it expedient, faked experiments which were supposed to train him in the knowledge of absolute truth.

Perhaps also it was because he started the fashion of taking everything tragically, so that everyone became pathetic — Saint-Preux[1], Julie[1], men, women and children. Farewell to simplicity, to comfort. Farewell to amusement, to play. Now we must speak with more passion than a Roman orator, we must exploit our emotions instead of concealing them, we must think in transports. Each passing epoch has its special quality which it believes eternal and superior to all past epochs, but it would seem to be the faults of Rousseau's time that were imposed on the children awaiting their turn on the world's stage. It was an epoch full of good intentions, of course, one that was more than ready to oppress young people in order to help them and make them happy.

Madame de Genlis was a disciple of Rousseau after her own fashion. She boasted that she was the very first woman to own a writing desk. Before her time women wrote prettily, wherever they could; afterwards they wrote solemnly, in state, at their desks. Madame de Genlis had a small body under all her finery and a tiny head under her powdered wig. She

[1] Characters in Rousseau's novel, *La Nouvelle Héloïse*, 1762.

would have preferred to appear more majestic. However, she made up for it by bearing herself with authority. In spite of appearances she had at heart only two ruling passions. The first was to shine, to cut a dash. Her childhood had seen a kind of prosperity. Her father was one of those men whose ideas are bigger than their purse. He had bought one estate after another on credit, so that he spent his life trying to pay for his châteaux, even going as far as Santo Domingo to seek his fortune. He was taken prisoner by the English, then set free, but died upon his return. When a man interprets life in this fashion, he does not bother his family much with his presence. His daughter, Stéphanie Félicité Ducrest, for that was her name, could, when she so desired, run about in the park of the unpaid-for château of Saint-Aubin-sur-Loire, climb trees, tear her frocks on the shrubbery, give free play to the vitality of her nature. But her mother liked society, as it is liked in the provinces rather than in Paris. In Paris it is liked with skepticism and in the provinces with conviction. Her daughter was just seven years old when, in an amateur play, she became a star that was never after content to cease shining. She played the role of Cupid in a performance given in honor of her father on one of his returns to the fold, and went about from then on garbed in pink silk, a quiver on her shoulder and blue wings on her back.

Accompanied by her mother, she sought her fortune in Paris. She became a virtuosa. She was one of those young ladies who play the harp in drawing rooms, who are feted, adulated, paid twenty-five louis an evening and forgotten the following morning—until the next triumph. She intended always to triumph and with no intervals. Married to Count de Genlis, she committed a thousand extravagances, such as smearing the good faces of the nuns with rouge at night in the convent where she lived while waiting for her husband's return from the army; playing the role of ghost to terrify the village folk; dressing like a man and riding astride along the highways; fitting herself out with a surgeon's kit and performing bloodlettings, and indulging in many other similar pleasant pastimes.

Madame de Genlis' other passion was pedagogy. As a little child she knew practically nothing, for they had given her a governess almost as ignorant as herself. By mutual consent they had given up the *Chronologie* of Père Buffier to read *Clélie*[1] and the *Théâtre* of Mademoiselle Barbier. She knew nothing, but she did not think it was necessary to know anything in order to teach. High up on the château terrace she played school with the little peasants gathered around her, holding their attention with promises of cakes and various other splendors. She was fine to behold in this new role, combining pedagogy and Cupid.

Joyfully she saw both passions combined and satisfied when the Duc de Chartres took a fancy to her, and made her his daughter's governess, when he even confided to her care the education of his sons. People made fun of her, that goes without saying. Paris and the court heaped up uncomplimentary epigrams; she was not unmindful of them. At least she would show them that she took her duties seriously. She had already published, in 1779, a *Théâtre à l'usage des jeunes*

[1] A romance by Mademoiselle de Scudéry, published in 1656.

personnes which contained plays written by her and acted by her daughters, Caroline and Pulchérie. In 1782 something quite different happened. She brought out a big book, *Adèle et Théodore,* or *Lettres sur l'éducation,* which had, alas, an enormous success not only in France but all over Europe.

What should children read? Fairy tales, as formerly? Certainly not. In the first place, tales are not moral and when it comes to morals Madame de Genlis does not compromise. Even if they were, it is not the moral of the story that the children would remember, but the descriptions of enchanted gardens and diamond palaces — as if diamond palaces existed in our lives! Such fantastic imaginings could give them only false ideas, retard the progress of their minds, and inspire them with disgust for really instructive reading. "I will give my children neither fairy tales nor *The Arabian Nights.* Even the tales that Madame d'Aulnoy wrote for that age are not suitable."

Poor children! Madame de Genlis has taken hold of them and will never let them go. To begin with, the entire house will be transformed into a classroom. The dining room will be decorated with Ovid's " Metamorphoses " painted in fresco; there will be conversation about mythology during luncheon, during dinner, as long as Jupiter rules the heavens. The square drawing room will be decorated with the " Chronology of Roman History," painted in oils on large canvases. There will also be medallions of the Roman kings, heroes who made the Republic illustrious, emperors up to Constantine. Opposite them there will be Roman ladies, Clelia, Cornelia, Portia and the empresses. Two other panels will represent selected scenes; and the spaces above the doors will also have their say, Roman history is so crowded! And so on. We spare you the other rooms and the staircase, which will have maps as its share of decoration. Everything will be in the same taste. Games will be arranged to serve as lessons. The magic lantern will no longer show Mr. Sun and Mrs. Moon, the servant drinking the wine she has drawn, or the baker's boy pulling the devil's tail, but instead, four or five hundred views taken from history will be shown with sound, appropriate commentary. Instead of castles made of cards, there will be exercises in architecture.

"Adèle and Théodore like to play at keeping house; through my care this game has become a veritable lesson in morals." How splendid! What would be the use of taking a walk if not to count the trees along the path, the pots of flowers on a terrace? Of what use the doll, if not for the sake of repeating to it the lessons a mother taught her daughter? Madame de Genlis was convinced that to safeguard the sensation of pleasure, to which children are susceptible, all that is needed is never to pronounce the word "study." If they once heard this fatal word, all was lost, the ruse was discovered. Otherwise, it was a perpetual cause for joy from morning to night that existence could conform so perfectly with the laws of nature, the dates of the Roman emperors and the geographic maps on the staircase.

There is no worthwhile book for children to read, states Madame de Genlis, Tutor; there is none in England, there is none in France. But at last the French are to possess such a treasure. Smilingly she holds out to them *Les Veillées du Château,* two years after she had given *Adèle et Théodore* to the world.

Three volumes made up of two thousand pages — no mean effort.

The title sounded hopeful. This is going to be like an old engraving: evenings before the hearth, the household gathered together; the servants permitted to sit near their masters while an old servant relates stories of bygone days. But Madame de Genlis would have had to change thoroughly and all at once. If there are to be stories she will relate them herself, behind the transparent mask of the Marquise de Clémire, who has retired to her château in Burgundy, with César her son, and her daughters Caroline and Pulchérie. If they have been very good, she will take a manuscript from the drawer and read to them. Oh, how boring they are, those readings that are supposed to be looked forward to impatiently and accepted as a treat! How inhuman! Not only because the characters who play the parts are nothing but puppets, but because, instead of virtue, they teach the fashionable conventions of the day; instead of charity, false simplicity and arrogance. Only the powerful and the rich are of importance. No child is worthy of our interest unless his father is a marquis or count, unless he owns a château, unless he has an *abbé* as instructor and servants to obey orders. Doing good meant mounting a platform in order to accomplish, with great pomp, a generous act that will be counted to his credit. We know, of course, that men are equal; that is a law established by Christ. But Madame de Genlis advances this reservation, that the manner in which one has been raised reëstablishes inequality among people. Servants who are not educated remain vulgar folk with whom one cannot mingle. The only persons with whom the sons of the family may associate without loss of dignity are peasants. The latter are in the habit of offering bread and milk to their young masters when hungry from a walk. They are humble; they grow red with emotion if one pays them the honor of speaking to them. Put in their place, and with no desire to rise above it, they play the inferior parts of those dull idyls in which the small gentlemen play the principal roles.

Down with imagination above everything! Hunted, pursued, how can it dare to show itself again? It tries, however, the rebel; it finds a way, timidly, of reclaiming its place, as we shall see.

After dinner, Madame de Clémire, having a letter to write, left the children in the drawing room with the *abbé*. It was the recreation hour. Fifteen minutes later Madame de Clémire came back. She noticed Caroline and Pulchérie seated in a corner reading.

"What is that you are reading?" said Madame de Clémire.

"Mama, it is a book that Mademoiselle Justine lent to us."

" Is Mademoiselle Justine capable of directing your reading? And besides, ought you to borrow books without my consent?"

" That is what I told these young ladies," broke in the *abbé*, who was playing chess at the other end of the room with the *curé*. " But they did not wish to believe me. Monsieur César is more reasonable, he is watching our chess game and reading *Le Journal de Paris*."

"Well," resumed Madame de Clémire, addressing her daughters, " what are you reading? "

"Mama, it is . . . *Le Prince Percinet et la Princesse Gracieuse*."

"A fairy tale! How can such reading please you?"

"Mama, it is wrong of me I know, but I confess that I like fairy tales."

"And why? "

"Because I like anything that is marvelous, extraordinary . . . metamorphoses, crystal palaces, gold and silver . . . all that enchants me."

There is no use in flaring up; here are your model children, the minute your back is turned, reading a tale lent to them by the chambermaid and admitting unblushingly that they enjoy it! But as Madame de Genlis is not one who will permit victory to turn into defeat, she is going to make a decisive effort. Her readers want something extraordinary; very well, she will give it to them. She will tell them the story of a young adventurer, a story full of marvels. They shall hear about a ball of fire that appears in the air, then divides into two rainbows; a rock that holds passers-by motionless, as if they had suddenly taken root; a rain of blood; a poison so violent that if put on the point of a needle and thrust into a mad bull the beast would fall dead; automatons that draw and sing; an electrified key, paralyzing the hand and arm of whoever touches it; various cyclones and earthquakes; a tree that starts bleeding; is that enough? Have you had your fill of wonders? Wait a moment. These are not wonders. All these phenomena are explicable, natural, fundamentally simple and moreover witnessed by more than a hundred authors from whom Madame de Genlis took the trouble of borrowing them. Mystery is not the word to be used here. Nothing is more common than a ball of fire appearing in the air — all travelers have seen them. A rock that holds passers-by as if they had taken root contains a magnet, nothing more. Imagination had soared. Madame de Genlis catches it and clips its wings. It will not leave the earth again for a long time.

Berquin

Those years were not good ones for the young of France. As though *Adèle et Théodore* and *Les Veillées du Château* were not enough, Berquin set about publishing, from January 1782 on, *L'Ami des Enfants*. Small in format, made for little hands to hold, it contained comedies, dialogues, tales, letters; and the first of every month a new number made its way about Paris and the provinces. This journal even reached the point where it supported its owner and had its own office at the corner of the *rue de l'Université* and the *rue du Bac*. Thereupon, Berquin, radiant, launched *L'Ami des Adolescents* with the same success. And then, in separate units, in books of every shape and size, in volumes illustrated and with gilt edges, in cheap editions, Berquin prevailed up to the very end of the nineteenth century.

Again fashion had changed; it was no longer a matter of merely being reasonable, it was important to have feelings. Men were overjoyed to discover in themselves a certain power of emotion that they had believed lost forever, and immediately exaggerated its purposes, as is their custom. They were proud of being good, of being simple, proud of not being proud. They showed off; all their gestures were for exhibition. They sniffed with self-satisfaction over every generous action, over every eloquent tirade. Delighted with the idea that they were chosen beings, capable of practicing virtue, they dramatized not only their public, but their private, existences.

Berquin was " the children's friend," as one may choose the role of noble father or of leading man. He was a vain little man, in a mawkish, pathetic sort of way. Listen to his friend and successor, Bouilly, who believes he brings out the importance of events in Berquin's life by writing of him in this vein:

We used to live in the same hotel; it was a lonely retreat near the *rue Montmartre*, looking out over some gardens. One day when we were talking under the trees, he of new productions that he was still considering, and I of the ardent desire I felt to imitate him, his friend Ginguené entered, breathless, announcing that the French Academy had just awarded Berquin the prize for usefulness. Berquin, who had in no way sought this triumph, could not, in spite of his modesty, help being flattered by it. His face, with its gentle and keen expression, flushed with deep emotion; he assured us frankly that this prize, awarded him so freely, was all the dearer to him as he believed he deserved it. It is a trait of real talent to be able to appreciate one's merits oneself; a man of noble candor can be just to himself without being suspected of vanity.

It all breathes of that particular era. Berquin is informed that he has been chosen as tutor to the son of Louis XVI. Immediately he adopts a pose: "Berquin grew pale with fright and allowed these words to escape him: 'I am lost, for I shall love this illustrious child.'" As it worked out, he was embittered by not having this illustrious child to love, by not being chosen as tutor; embittered by being suspect, by being considered a Girondist, by no longer being greeted by the people in his district, by losing his popularity with the youngsters. And without even obtaining the glory of mounting the guillotine, he died, saddened, like an actor abandoned by his public.

He had started off by writing idyls and ballads. He continued, but in a minor key. He exploited pity. Then since optimism was the rage at this moment, he wanted to persuade children that everything is for the best in this best of worlds, and pointed out triumphantly that summer is a delicious season, autumn is perfect, winter is perfect; and that it is very wrong to say that one is cold when one is freezing, or that it is damp when it rains. He pointed out, since altruism was also the rage at that time, that it was far better to love poverty, to scorn riches, than to be an owner of property, and have the bother of keeping up castles, parks, crops and vineyards. That it is useless as well as unpleasant to own a gold watch, and that a little girl is just as happy (or should be) with an old silver one. He pointed out, in a comedy, that it is better to be restrained than to be free. Allow children to be the masters of their own time, let them eat the dishes they like, play the games they choose themselves, and scourges will then rain down upon them; they will fight with their neighbors, stuff themselves like gluttons, suffer from indigestion, fall into the river, think they are about to die. And afterwards, when their parents tell them they are going to give them their freedom, the children will tremble.

As he championed the good of humanity in general, but reduced humanity to the aristocracy (which he reverenced even more than did Madame de Genlis, who at least belonged to it), he named his actors Monsieur de Milfort, Monsieur de Valcourt, Monsieur de Courcy, Mademoiselle Agathe de Saint-Félix, Mademoiselle Dorothée de Louvreuil. Small sirs bow respectfully before small ladies; there are curtsies and compliments. All ills fall upon the poor, whose role it is to make evident the pocket-book generosity of the rich man. The father dies, the mother is ill, a child has broken its leg. The family is perishing of hunger and, whenever possible, it is cold. The poor shiver, and are really not properly poor unless surrounded by snow and ice. Then appear the little rich children, who, with aureole and halo, solemnly offer their alms. Benefactors and benefited form a group as though in a Greuze painting; emotion is at its height.

While reading Berquin, we can seem to hear a kind of antiquated tune constantly off-key. Nothing is simple, nothing is natural, nothing is real. He exaggerates his characters. If a child is naughty, he will depict him as cowardly, greedy, insolent, quarrelsome, thieving, all at the same time. If a child is fickle, he will be shown giving up, one after the other and quick as a wink, drawing, Italian, Spanish, English, German, dancing, the violin and the flute. And that is by no means all. Conversions are speedy and thorough. Agathe was vain, peevish, hurt everyone without caring, but was insulted by the slightest familiarity shown to herself. All at once she becomes so simple, sympathetic, agreeable that she wins all hearts. He exaggerates grandiloquence. Listen to the terms in which Léonor addresses the wicked Robert, in " Colin Maillard," one of the stories in *L'Ami des Enfants:*

Your excuses and your genuflexions are of an insolent irony that I despise. But even were they sincere, scarcely would they suffice to atone for your dishonest conduct, and had I not regarded all that as a joke, and an extremely coarse one to be sure, I am well aware what action I would already have taken. I beg you with insistence, Monsieur, no longer to permit yourself jests of this nature, lest we may no longer remain together.

The children that Berquin presents to us love the subjunctive, and he presents them with tears in his voice. Teachers weep because a little girl has been naughty, but before long these bitter tears turn into sobs of joy because she is good again. Young Edouard de Bellecombe, a boarding pupil at the Ecole Militaire, refuses his usual lunch and insists upon eating only stale bread. The officers who govern the school are amazed; they want to force Edouard to do as his comrades do. They have all their trouble for nothing. He replies only with tears when asked for an explanation and already these tears are contagious. The *Directeur* presents his report to the *Gouverneur*:

Le Gouverneur:

What is this you are telling me? This child must be of Spartan birth!

Le Directeur:

Granted. But here where no peculiarities are permitted, where the training of a soldier implies submission to the general subordination, I feared that his example might prove dangerous to the others. A dozen times I have wanted to urge or compel him to eat what was put before him; he replied to my pleas and orders only by gazing at me with eyes filled with pathetic tears. . . . Forgive me, Monsieur, I believe I am weeping myself. . . .

Le Gouverneur:

I too feel overcome by your account.

When everything is explained in the end, when we learn that Edouard eats dry bread because his father, a former lieutenant of the King but without a pension, is in the most dire misery and has nothing to eat but bread, and when this unhappy father at last obtains his pension, I leave you to imagine how everyone weeps, and with what delight. A certain Monsieur de Valcourt, in " *Un bon cœur fait pardonner bien des étourderies,*" another story in *L'Ami des Enfants,* dries sometimes one eye and sometimes the other, as if each eye claimed the right to weep separately in its own behalf. Or let us admire this attitude in *"Le bouquet qui ne se flétrit jamais"*:

I could say no more, but she felt clearly what was happening in my heart. Her trembling arms pressed me against her bosom with a tenderness that I am unable to portray to you. I felt her tears flowing on my face whilst her eyes were turned heavenward.

Can it be that Berquin does not understand children? He must have looked at them occasionally before depicting them. He sees them as they are at birth — red, crying, their limbs frail and brittle, their heads soft as cotton. He knows how much love must be placed at their service before they are able to walk, to speak, or even to feed themselves. He is familiar with their traits, their faults, their ways. He knows that little girls show signs of coquetry, and boys of pugnacity, at an early age; that they live in a world of their own, very different from the grown-up one, where grownups are less important than they think themselves to be. Several of his comedies lack neither vivacity nor dramatic movement. Indeed, how could his success be explained if he had not had some hold on readers?

But believing himself to be the best of men, the only moral he ever suggested to them was that of the Pharisee who prayed God to make his brother as perfect as he was. All that he was capable of doing, at his very best, was to mold the children's minds in a form that would enable them to exist painlessly in a society already doomed to perish. Near-sighted, he could not distinguish between that which endures and that which passes, confusing the transitory with the eternal.

"What sweet encouragement for my heart," said Berquin, "when I consider the thousands of beings now growing up who are devoted to my memory." This is only too true; thousands of young people have read him, thousands of young people have been gently oppressed by him. Nor do we have the consolation of believing that his was an exceptional case, or that of a few authors only or of merely one country; or that France, because her habit of clear, straight thinking may make over-rigid disciplinarians, is alone guilty. Let us cross the Channel and we shall see how history repeats itself in England, where a lovely dawn was speedily obscured; a holiday scarcely begun changed swiftly into tasks and lessons. And where many rapacious English women were only waiting to fling themselves upon the children!

John Newbery's Bookshop

What a charming idea it was to create a bookshop, not for adults who already have as many as they could wish, but for boys and girls. A bookshop which would allow them to come in and browse among its shelves, to play at being grown-up clients who can hardly decide what they want where there is so much to choose from; to carry home proudly books composed, printed and illustrated just for them. It was a wonderful day when John Newbery of London, braving prejudices and gossip, hoisted up over his shop the daring sign, "Juvenile Library." A bookshop for you, young ladies and gentlemen.

This happened about 1750. For a long time there had been hornbooks. Imagine a sheet of paper on which are printed the alphabet, numbers up to ten, and a prayer. Imagine this placed in a frame with a handle, like the menus in our cheap restaurants, and covered over with a sheet of horn transparent enough to read through, but sturdy enough to protect the paper from finger marks, and there you have the model hornbook. As time went on, it wanted to change, to enlarge, to be less crude, to dress itself up with pictures. The alphabet asked to be included in the tales, where it could appear easily, yet without being too evident, and where it would make a better showing than in this frame with a handle, which was a real humiliation.

There were also chapbooks, books that pedlars carried in their packs and sold to the people, to those anyway who knew how to read, just as the volumes of the *Bibliothèque Bleue* were peddled in France. The legends of Antiquity, of the Middle Ages, all the old romantic material of which men never weary, suffered from their crude appearance, with poor type and cheap paper. *The History of Thomas Hickathrift, The Babes in the Wood, Bevis of Southampton,* and other stories of local interest were also clamoring for better presentation.

There were childish rhymes, too, that clung in everyone's memory, born near the cradle, learned by boys and girls who were taught by their mothers; verses that asked nothing better than to have a permanent place and see themselves gathered together in book form.

John Newbery understood that from all these old things he could make something new. He remodeled, simplified, expurgated. He employed purveyors and writers able to understand the spirit of the undertaking; who could not only make use of the source material, but were also creative themselves. Most important of all, he made books more beautiful, using good paper, amusing pictures, fine bindings, and gilt edges.

Imagine two shop windows with small panes of glass; in the middle a door wide open and, in front of his books, John Newbery, the owner of the Juvenile Library, ready and waiting to inform and to serve. As he is not very certain that such unusual commerce will win his bread for him, he also sells remedies — powders to prevent fever, tablets to cure colic, balm, and even the elixir of life. Anyone, however, can sell remedies, but so far no one else has sold books for children. There is a whole collection to choose from; some for a penny, twopence, sixpence, a shilling. Does sandy-haired Tommy or small Mary with her golden curls want the story " Old Zig Zag "[1] and the horn that he used to understand the language of birds, beasts, fishes, insects? Or *Pretty Poems for Children Three Feet High*? Or the *Lilliputian Magazine*? Or Fables? Or Fairy Tales? Let them feel at home; they have only to help themselves. John Newbery offers them works that he has prepared for them and dedicates to them: " To all those who are good this book is dedicated by their best friend."

Make no mistake in the address. There is another Newbery at the corner of Saint Paul's Churchyard and Ludgate Street, but that one has nothing in common with John Newbery, the real, the only bookseller for children. The other Newbery sells books to grownups, much good may it do him! The real John Newbery is at number 65 Saint Paul's Churchyard, at the sign of the Bible and Sun.

[1] In *The Valentine's Gift.* 1777.

If they had not been careful about the right address they would have shown real ingratitude. In Old England, from then on, there was a child literature which, or so it seemed, had only to develop itself freely. Heroes in miniature, whose only role in life was to delight children with their spontaneity, gaiety and life, escaped from the kindly bookseller's shop and peopled all their dreams. Giles Gingerbread was one of them, he who liked books so much that he swallowed their words.

Then there was Tommy Trip,[1] not much taller than Tom Thumb, but who is far superior. First of all, he knows how to read, having learned his letters, the letters of the hornbook that have been slipped into his story so that others may learn them also. Tommy Trip is never separated from his dog, the faithful Jouler, who serves him as steed. Mounted on Jouler, Tommy Trip travels through the streets of London. He stops at every door to see what the children are doing. If they are good, he leaves them an apple, an orange, or a sweetmeat, and off he goes again at a gallop. He's a brave one. The giant Woglog torments a child. Tommy Trip darts out, challenges him, beats him up and returns victor. No one was dearer to the hearts of English children than Tommy Trip, except possibly Goody Two Shoes.

" Philosophers, politicians and necromancers, and men learned in every subject are begged to observe that the first of January, that is to say New Year's Day (Oh! If only we could all start a new year!) Mr. Newbery intends to publish certain important vol-

[1] "Adventures of Tommy Trip and and his Dog Jouler " in *Lilliputian Magazine,* issued not in monthly numbers, but as a book, in 1752.

umes, bound and gilded, and consequently invites all his little friends who are good to come and ask for them at the Bible and Sun; but those who are naughty shall not have any." Thus the philosophic bookseller announces to the world, in the year 1765, the appearance of *Goody Two Shoes*, also called *Margery Two Shoes* or *Margot les Deux Souliers*. She was called that because she was so poor that she never had more than one shoe at a time, so she was unable to control her joy when, one day, someone gave her a whole pair. She went about showing her treasured shoes to all the village folk and crying out: "Two shoes! Two shoes!" It was a triumph. People argued over the story of *Goody Two Shoes*, printed, John Newbery declared, from an original manuscript found in the Vatican at Rome, with drawings by Michelangelo.

And now let us skip a generation; Newbery is dead but his shop is still open. Along comes Charles Lamb, charming soul, both ironic and tender; Charles Lamb and his sister Mary, vibrant with all the anguish and joy of the spirit, who, in search of books for children, conceive the idea of coming to the famous bookshop. They enter; they ask the clerk for *Goody Two Shoes;* and the clerk has the greatest trouble in the world finding a copy of it way over in a corner. On the other hand, the shop is full of books by Mrs. Barbauld and Mrs. Trimmer, heaps of them. And Charles Lamb, who relates this fact to Coleridge in a letter which he wrote to him in 1802, condemns soundly Mrs. Barbauld and Mrs. Trimmer. Devil take them! cries he. These idiotic women and their crew have brought rust and pestilence to everything human in men and children! Whence this explosion of anger? And what is this change?

Juvenile literature had gone astray. People had taken a few ideas from Locke and Rousseau, mixed them up with more or less of puritan sentiment, a little rationalism, and from this strange leaven sprouted a quantity of works that, on the decline of the century, were installed in the place of honor in the shop window of the late John Newbery. They were inspired, first of all, by the idea that there was not a single hour in the child's life but must be consecrated to usefulness. Like Madame de Genlis, but with this difference, that the English are more tenacious, more obstinate and more formidable. The French often stop along the way, but nothing stops the English once they have started; they are slow but intrepid.

To admire an oak for its beauty is time wasted. Tell me of a book that trains children at once to calculate what the oak can yield cut up into planks. We cannot even imagine to what point of perfection this method can lead us.

Let us take, for example, a little boy and girl who, on a fine morning in early summer, go down to the garden to gather strawberries.

A little while after dinner, Harry and Lucy went with their mother into the garden; and Lucy was desired to gather six strawberries, and Harry was desired to gather four strawberries. And when they were put together, Harry counted them and found that they made ten. Lucy was not obliged to count them, for she knew by rote, or by heart, as it is sometimes called, that six and four make ten.

Each of them then brought five strawberries; and Harry knew, without counting, that when they were put together, they would make ten. And Lucy knew that the parcel of strawberries which they gathered first, which made ten,

34

would, when added to the second parcel, which also consisted of ten, make twenty.

They now went and gathered ten more. One gathered three, and the other gathered seven; and this ten, added to the former, made thirty. And they went again and brought ten more to their mother. This ten was made up of eight and two; and this ten, added to the thirty they had gathered before, made forty.[1]

Here was a way of teaching arithmetic without seeming to do so. What skill! What charm! What joy! No doubt that, influenced by such literature, children would grow into the most solid, the most practical of human beings; the only qualities that were important and that satisfied man's nature fully.

Nothing more was needed but a sense of morality, a morality thoroughly understood. It must be severe and unrelenting. Every mistake must be punished at once and without pity. Let children prick themselves with thorns to teach them that thorns prick; burn themselves with sealing wax to teach them that wax burns; hurt their feet dangerously to teach them that they should prefer to buy a good solid pair of shoes rather than the elegant slippers which they see displayed in the stores. Set in motion these different trials which all, every one of them, end in well-earned afflictions. Show them that, on the other hand, every good action is immediately rewarded by a profit which makes it more advantageous than the best kind of bank transaction. If a small boy has lost some nuts, and you happen to bring them back to him, he will bring back to you the cherries that you had lost. An eye for an eye. If you encounter a little chimney sweep who looks unhappy, do not hesitate to give him

[1] From "Harry and Lucy" in *Easy Lessons* by Maria Edgeworth.

alms, for you may possibly pass again through the same village, your horse may rear and throw you into the water. Then the little chimney sweep will pull you out of the water. You will have spent only a few pennies and you will make a profit by escaping death. Consider such a dividend!

Let us look over the famous books that inspired a host of others, even more foolish, even less human. Try, if you can, to read them; attempt it at least as an adventure. Open the masterpiece of Thomas Day, who was one of the initiators of the genre; a man so dreadfully serious, says one of his critics, that no one ever saw him smile during his life — with the result that, after his death, no one ever spoke of him without smiling. A man of ideas, he had, among others, the idea of taking two young girls, one an orphan and the other a foundling, and having them raised according to his pedagogical principles in order to choose one of them later for an ideal wife. As a matter of fact, he married neither of them. He also had the idea of bringing out a book that would serve as a model and also bring delight to the younger generation.

Courage! Once upon a time there was a perfectly detestable spoiled child, called Thomas Merton, the son of a rich middle-class couple who settled in England after making a fortune in the West Indies. The son of a farmer neighbor, named Harry Sandford, rescues Thomas Merton from a snake that was about to bite him. This Sandford is a boy full of admirable qualities, developed in him by the pastor, Mr. Barlow, who is the village schoolmaster. Instantly Mr. Merton Senior places his son in the hands of Mr. Barlow, along with Sandford. And Mr. Barlow, for hundreds of pages, pours out on them the pitiless floods of his eloquence and wisdom, and Thomas Merton loses his faults and becomes the most perfect young gentleman who has ever lived under the English sky. Such is *Sandford and Merton*[1], which appeared from 1783 to 1789, and which innumerable masters have made innumerable children swallow.

Shall we call forth, from the realm of shades where the maledictions of Charles Lamb pursue her, the intrepid Mrs. Trimmer? She can intercede for herself, to be sure, with her *Story of Robin Red Breast*. But how sharp she was! And aggressive! With what ferocity she pursued in general all those who were not of her opinion and, in particular, those wicked French writers, faithless and lawless creatures, without morals and without shame — liars, wasters, atheists and corrupters of youth! With what pious fury she wished eternal damnation on unfortunate sinners! How she spoke up not only to the philosophers, but to the papists, longing to throw them all together into a good hell-fire. But, even so, we might forgive her clamor and her complaints if she had any attractive quality. But she is odious to read, and her wordy writings bore us to death.

Shall we evoke Mrs. Barbauld? She starts out to depict for us the gentle pleasures of *Evenings at Home*. She opens up a portfolio and takes out the first instructive and moral tale. That is enough: beware of what is to come; let us flee. There is a whole battalion of these fearsome women: Hannah More, Mary Wollstonecraft, who undertook to transform young girls into essentially reasonable creatures; Maria Edgeworth, less excusable than all the others. When she gave up mixing pedagogy and literature, she was not

[1] *The History of Sandford and Merton* by Thomas Day.

37

lacking in talent. But as soon as she wanted to instruct and amuse at the same time she became hopeless:

There was a little boy whose name was Frank. He had a father and a mother, who were very kind to him; and he loved them. He liked to talk to them, and he liked to walk with them, and he liked to be with them. He liked to do what they asked him to do; and he took care not to do what they desired him not to do. When his father or mother said to him, " Frank, shut the door," he ran directly and shut the door. When they said to him, " Frank, do not touch that knife," he took his hands away from the knife and did not touch it. He was an obedient little boy.[1]

We regret deeply that the parents of little Frank never forbade him to read Maria Edgeworth.

In Germany

Over a long period of time in Germany there were no books produced for children. Goethe himself mentions this fact in connection with his own first adventures in reading[2]:

At that time there were not yet any libraries for children. Adults . . . simply passed their own culture along to those who were to follow in their steps.

Aside from the *Orbis Pictus* of Amos Comenius, no book of this kind fell into our hands; but we often turned the pages of the folio Bible with Mérian's copper engravings; Gottfried's *La Chronique*, with illustrations by the same master, taught us the most wonderful facts of universal history; *L'Acerra Philologica* added to this all kinds of fables, mythological tales, and strange items; and as I soon became familiar with Ovid's *Metamorphoses* and studied zealously the first books especially, my young brain was speedily filled

[1] From " Frank " in *Easy Lessons* by Maria Edgeworth.
[2] *Dichtung und Wahrheit*, Book 1.

with a mass of pictures and adventures, forms, important and admirable events; and I was never bored, applying myself more and more to working, reviewing and using over and over again all this acquired knowledge. The *Telemachus* of Fénelon produced on us an effect far more salutary and moral than did all the gross and dangerous antiquated stuff that prevailed in our daily lives. In the natural course of events the story of *Robinson Crusoe* was given to us. . . . The Voyage of Admiral Anson around the world combined the dignity of the real with the imaginative richness of a story, and in our minds we accompanied this good sailor far off into the wide world, trying to follow him with our finger on the globe.

I discovered a still more abundant harvest, when I came across a mass of writings, which in their natural form could not be qualified as excellent, but whose content has however had the merit of bringing the past close to us in an ingenious way. The house that published, or, it would be better to say, manufactured these books which later were to become famous and even illustrious under the title of *Popular Writings, Popular Books,* was at Frankfort. Because of their large output they were printed in stereotype on the most wretched paper and were almost illegible. We children had the joy of finding these precious remnants of the Middle Ages, spread out every day in front of a bookshop, and of being able to own them for a few *kreutzers*. *Eulenspiegel, Les Quatre Fils Aymon, Le Belle Mélusine, L'Empereur Octavien, Fortunatus,* and the whole sequel up to *The Wandering Jew,* were at our disposition. We had this great advantage, too, that when we had worn out or ruined one of these books, we could quickly procure another and ruin it all over again.

Finally, after great labor, a literature for children[1] was born. But first there had to be an awakening of

[1] H. L. Koester, *Geschichte der deutschen Jugendliteratur,* 4th ed., 1927.

feeling, of emotion, of the consciousness of the rights of the individual, a complete change in point of view, as well as a complete change in pedagogy, before an effort could be made to introduce some element of pleasure in reading matter for children. Basedow, the friend of man, had a part to play also. He it was who had aroused an innovator, Christian Felix Weisse, who, being himself the father of a large family, had published in 1765 songs for his own children and those of others. Weisse experimented with an ABC crammed with pleasant tidbits; after which he launched a newspaper, *Der Kinderfreund,* which made him popular throughout Germany in the year 1775; and in 1784 there was a sequel to it, *Briefwechsel der Familie des Kinderfreundes.* After that there was no stopping him.

But we have to admit that Basedow, even if he had pedagogic genius, was lacking in literary genius; that Christian Felix Weisse, even if he was capable of making verses, was incapable of writing poetry; and that the titles alone of his little poems have something discouraging about them: " O dear and sweet diligence"; "Ah! How I would like to be amiable! " "Arise, little lazy one "; " My child, copy the bee." Facing such inducements, who would not take fright? *Der Kinderfreund* seems extremely unreadable to us; the Father, the Mother, the Children are about as natural as family portraits or wax mannequins. And what is there to be said for Master Philotechnos, Dr. Chronickel, Monsieur Papillon, and Spirite, the poet? Let them alone, take your flight again and as swiftly as possible because, by following this road, we would meet their successors and imitators who are even worse. Anybody who knew merely how to hold a pen, anybody who wanted to earn a little money in a relatively honest way, anybody who felt an attraction for beloved youth, always a good customer, concocted edifying stories. Virtue was never praised so much; useful advice was never so freely given; adolescence was never urged more eagerly to improve itself by means of readings which were to transform it instantaneously and unsuspectingly. Every market day at Leipzig brought to shore, like a tidal wave, countless quantities of books for possible buyers; but as a contemporary puts it, neither pearls nor amber were found there, only empty shells. The illustrators are not included in these comments, for the pictures are often superior to the text. But that is an entirely different study, and is not our subject here.

Everything is mixed together and everywhere, at about the same time, we witness the same failure. Basedow, Weisse and the other Germans imitated Madame Leprince de Beaumont. Berquin imitated, as far as he could, *Der Kinderfreund* of Weisse, translated Thomas Day, translated Sarah Trimmer. Sarah Trimmer admired and emulated the works of Madame de Genlis, esteemed equally by Maria Edgeworth. The English translated Berquin as they had translated *Adèle et Théodore* and *Les Veillées du Château*. This tasteless food, exported from one country to another, was offered to all the children of Europe. At the end of the eighteenth century, and in the first years of the nineteenth, a literature developed that, while made expressly for children, seemed to ignore what they liked and asked for, and to deny them many of their most marked preferences, to such an extent that now, after a hundred years have passed, it seems like a vast rubbish heap.

What Are Good Books?

Liberators will come, from Grimm to Andersen; and there will be others later on, but before them, beside them, around them, how many pedants and fools there were! How many exploiters trying to make a profit from worthless merchandise! What a cemetery!

You may say: It is all very well to look disgusted. What does please you, anyway, and just what are you asking for? Stories, nothing but stories? Do you grow angry as soon as knowledge or morals is mentioned? And for a book to satisfy you, must it contain absolutely nothing? First of all, I reply, there are good books of every kind; and when one of them is good, even though it does not contain what I ask for, let it be welcomed gratefully. I will enumerate the kind of books which seem to me good.

I like books that remain faithful to the very essence of art; namely, those that offer to children an intuitive and direct way of knowledge, a simple beauty capable of being perceived immediately, arousing in their souls a vibration which will endure all their lives.

And those that provide them with pictures, the kind that they like; pictures chosen from the riches of the whole world; enchanting pictures that bring release and joy, happiness gained before reality closes in upon them, insurance against the time, all too soon, when there will be nothing but realities.

And books that awaken in them not maudlin sentimentality, but sensibility; that enable them to share in great human emotions; that give them respect for universal life — that of animals, of plants; that teach them not to despise everything that is mysterious in creation and in man.

And books which respect the valor and eminent dignity of play; which understand that the training of intelligence and of reason cannot, and must not, always have the immediately useful and practical as its goal.

I like books of knowledge; not those that want to encroach upon recreation, upon leisure, pretending to be able to teach anything without drudgery. There is no truth in that. There are things which cannot be learned without great pains; we must be resigned to it. I like books of knowledge when they are not just grammar or geometry poorly disguised; when they have tact and moderation; when, instead of pouring out so much material on a child's soul that it is crushed, they plant in it a seed that will develop from the inside. I like them when they do not deceive themselves about the quality of knowledge, and do not claim that knowledge can take the place of everything else. I like them especially when they distill from all the different kinds of knowledge the most difficult and the most necessary — that of the human heart.

A Perrault, while he is relating marvels to us, teaches us with wit and charm not to be mistaken about men, women and children; he is full of observation and he is never ponderous. He has so many delightful traits, so just and so true, that they penetrate the soul deeply; so full of strength that they will ripen gradually in the spirit to blossom some day into wisdom! In "Hop o' My Thumb": "She was indeed poor, but she was their mother." "This Peter was her eldest son whom she loved above all the rest, because he was somewhat carroty, as she herself was." "It is quite possible that the woodcutter was more

43

vexed than his wife, but she kept teasing him and he felt as many other people do who admire women who say the right thing, but find extremely tiresome those who never say anything but the right thing." In " Puss in Boots ": " The King lavished caresses upon him, and as the fine garments he had given him enhanced his good looks (for he was well made and very handsome) the King's daughter found him very much to her taste and the Marquis de Carabas had no sooner cast two or three glances towards her, very respectfully and tenderly, than she fell madly in love with him." In the story of " The Sleeping Beauty," who has been asleep for a hundred years, and whose first words, when she wakens and sees before her a charming prince, are: "Is it you, my prince? I have waited long for you to come." These tales, as Fénelon said of poetry, are more useful and more serious than common persons realize.

Finally, I like books that contain a profound morality. Not the kind of morality which consists in believing oneself a hero because one has given two cents to a poor man, or which names as characteristics the faults peculiar to one era, or one nation; here snivelling pity, there a pietism that knows nothing of charity; somewhere else a middle class hypocrisy. Not the kind of morality that asks for no deeply felt consent, for no personal effort, and which is nothing but a rule imposed willy-nilly by the strongest. I like books that set in action truths worthy of lasting forever, and of inspiring one's whole inner life; those demonstrating that an unselfish and faithful love always ends by finding its reward, be it only in oneself; how ugly and low are envy, jealousy and greed; how people who utter only slander and lies end by coughing up vipers and toads whenever they speak. In short, I like books that have the integrity to perpetuate their own faith in truth and justice. Listen once more to what Perrault says to us:

Is it not praiseworthy of fathers and mothers, when the children are not yet old enough to taste strong unpleasant truths, to make them like them, and if I may put it this way, to make them swallow them by enveloping them in tales that are pleasant and suited to their tender years? It is unbelievable how eagerly these innocent souls, whose natural goodness has not yet been corrupted, receive these subtle teachings. We see them sad and depressed as long as the hero or the heroine is unlucky, and shouting with joy when the time for their happiness arrives; in the same way, having endured impatiently the prosperity of the wicked man or woman, they are overjoyed when they see them finally punished as they deserve.

I know very well that these conditions are difficult to fulfil. They are even more imperative than when it is a question of a good book for men, which in itself is not so easy to produce. But to misshape young souls, to profit by a certain facility that one may possess to add to the number of indigestible and sham books, to give oneself too easily the airs of a moralist and scholar, to cheat in quality — that is what I call oppressing children.

II

CHILDREN HAVE DEFENDED
THEMSELVES

Robinson Crusoe

W E needn't worry; children do not let themselves be oppressed without resistance. We wish to dominate, but they wish to be free: the result is a grand battle. In vain we offer them a book which seems to us full of admirable qualities, a book designed to make them more knowing than Pico della Mirandola and wiser than Solomon. Just as they used to turn away from the watch when its tick-tick no longer interested them, so they turn with an air of disgust from the book offered to them. The booksellers are aware of this as they gaze sadly about their shop at the number of works put there to tempt their young clients, and which their young clients refuse to approach. Indeed, they would sell very few of them if it were not for the uncles and aunts, the godfathers and godmothers, who buy them as presents and surprises because the title of the work is promising or the clerk recommends it. But the nephews and godsons are not so gullible. Politeness compels them to accept, but no force in the world can compel them to read. It is their way of defense, and they make good use of it. What precocious skill they have for skipping paragraphs, pages, whole chapters! A glance of the eye, a thrust of the thumb, is all they need. They sense the coming of a sermon and skip it dexterously.

To tell the truth, I admire them. We always hesitate, we men, to throw a book in the wastebasket because it bores us. If we suppressed everything that bored us, what would our life become! Our habits are formed and we are so resigned that it seems as though a little boredom is necessary to real admiration. So we keep on courageously, waiting for the consoling page, even reproaching ourselves for our yawns. But the children are ruthless.

You, Madame de Genlis, Berquin, will attain the top shelf, the one that can be reached only with a ladder, and from there you will pass on to the attic. And you also, you English women, who thought you had won eternal glory because you were so full of self-confidence, you will pass on to the attic, and no one will read you any more, except the curious, who, to their own misfortune, seek to find out how men have fooled themselves in the course of their journey which leads them God knows where. And you also, you Germans, who went ahead only after having reasoned everything out meticulously and who owed everything to method, especially your mistakes. The children are as finished with you as they are with crinolines or pantaloons. You will go the same way, you innumerable authors who have featured, who still feature, in the distribution of prizes. Your sole chance of being read lasts only five minutes, while the pupil reaches his bench and believes himself obliged to open you; he will never do so again. Books with over-showy gilding and a red that fades, you smell of the distribution of prizes, and with one glance you are condemned. Your reputation is made, you have fooled too many generations.

Children defend themselves, I tell you. They manifest at first a degree of inertia that resists the liveliest attacks; finally they take the offensive and expel their false friends from a domain in which they wish to remain the rulers. Nothing is done to create a common opinion among them and yet that opinion exists. They would be wholly incapable of defining the faults that displease them; but they cannot be made to believe that a book which displeases them *should* please them in spite of themselves. Whatever their differences may be as to age, sex, or social position, they detest with common accord disguised sermons, hypocritical lessons, irreproachable little boys and girls who behave with more docility than their dolls. It is as though they sensed obscurely the vanity and danger of exterior constraints, as though they brought into the world with them a spontaneous hatred of the insincere and the false. The adults insist, the children pretend to yield and do not yield. We overpower them; they rise up again. Thus does the struggle continue, in which the weaker will triumph.

It is the law. This newborn babe who wails in his swaddling clothes will end by dominating the whole household, which will obey him and submit to his tyranny. Bearded giants, bending over his cradle, will assume an unnatural tone of voice trying to make

49

themselves understood, and will lisp in his honor. As soon as he begins to talk, his parents will imitate his language. He will give them ridiculous and tender names which they will be thrilled to accept, and which they will cherish the length of their days, so that strangers, not in on the secret, will be astonished to hear old men calling each other by childish pet names.

Victor Hugo is at the height of his glory. The people of Paris take off their hats before him when he passes through the streets. He lacks none of the satisfactions of self-esteem or of pride. Even those who criticize and attack him start off by rendering homage to his genius. In his own eyes, he is the oracle, the prophet, the demigod. He has not only revised French letters, he has invented a philosophy, a religion; he has heard the inner voice. Now it happens that his grandson calls him Papapa; and so he becomes Papapa for the whole household. Such is the victory of the child. Everybody will exert himself to the utmost in his service. The father will yield up his dignity as head of the family and will no longer hold any but second rank in the affection of the mother. Each event in the life of the newcomer will take on the quality of an important occasion—his first tooth, his first trousers. Soon there will be no other birthday but his. He will have to have better food than that which was good enough for his parents, and finer clothes. He will go on, from conquest to conquest, until the day when he himself, leaving the world of children to enter the world of grownups, becomes a father in his turn, and sees his own sons rule over him.

Children reject the books that do not treat them as equals and which call them " dear little readers "; the books which do not respond to their own nature, which do not attract their eye through pictures, or their spirit by liveliness; books which teach them only what they can learn at school, books which put them to sleep but not to dream. But inversely, when they have singled out a work that they like and have decided to take possession of it, nothing can make them change their minds. They may not know how to feed or clothe themselves without a long apprenticeship, but they are extremely persistent. It is that book there that they want, that very one and not its neighbor. And they all want it, the whole lot of them. They seize it, hold on to it, put their mark on it, make it their own. If the story is not written for them, that is a detail which does not concern them; they attach no importance to it, unless they see in that an added charm.

I maintain that they have won by main force the best and the most famous of their favorite books. Their authors were addressing themselves to men, but it is the children who have taken possession of them.

There was a grouchy, morose, old man who, of all beings on earth, seemed least destined to please children. It is true that he had eight sons and daughters— but sons shift for themselves and the duty to daughters is fulfilled if they are given a dowry when they marry; and they do not hesitate to ask for it, the hussies! So reasoned the old Defoe. How did he happen to write for other people's children, not cherishing his own?

First of all, he wrote to earn money; and to make people continue to talk about him as they had done during the period of his strength. How they had extolled, criticized, slandered, scorned, admired him! Such experiences are not forgotten, and even when he decided to retire he wanted his name to keep on resounding, at least in the London bookshops and cafés. He wrote to confess, to vent the overflow of an activity even old age could not exhaust. He addressed himself to gentlemen, to the middle class, to merchants whose ships did business in every part of the world, to women who shivered at the recital of high adventures; to everybody except to children.

No, indeed, he had no intention of becoming one of those teachers, those pedagogues who wipe the noses of little brats in the London schools. His family wanted him to be a pastor, and he doubtless did well to pay no attention to their zeal. He certainly had a hatred of papism, a horror of the established church, a tendency to moralize and lecture come what may. But he was never able to distinguish clearly between the conceptions of good and evil. He was a merchant, not one of those who practice the dull virtues of order and economy and who spend their lives working meanly behind a counter. He was fond of gambling, of strokes of genius, of speculations that made it possible to win or lose a fortune in a flash; he liked money for spending. He was ostentatious and, even during his rich periods, always worried and in need. But his greatest passion was politics. To embrace a cause, to uphold it, to publish a newspaper which sets forth its opinion every morning, to launch tracts and pamphlets that wound the enemy in a sensitive spot, to repay violence with violence, to provoke insult, to turn each day as it came along into a battle field, that was joy! That was living! A profession has its vicissitudes; today he is in power, a favorite with the great and the King. The King dies, power changes hands; suddenly he falls from grace and because of a pamphlet that displeases the authorities he is placed in the pillory, as was the case in the year 1703. Even then he was lucky, when tied to the stake in the public square, not to be covered with insults and spit upon, but applauded and acclaimed; for the crowd that day was with him. It was not always with him. The slope is dangerous: little by little he begins to think only of the effect produced, of the noise, of the success, of the money, without thinking of the nature of the cause that he is defending; he even defends two contrary causes, at first one after the other, finally both at the same time. He becomes a secret agent, a spy, and then is betrayed. So he finds himself, towards sixty, rather badly off. He leaves London, gives up a fight in which he is too old to figure in the front rank; he settles down in the country, retires. . . .

No, not yet. When one is named Daniel Defoe, there is no real retirement except death. He schemes, deals in obscure affairs, warms up his blood arguing with his daughters. To provide the comfort which seems of prime necessity to him, he takes up his pen once more and becomes a novelist. The story of Selkirk, that sailor who lived for four years and four months on the island of Juan Fernandez, who became half savage and was one of the sights of London on his return there — here was a theme to rouse his mettle! Writing without rereading, finishing his book as though it were a task, done solely in order that the publisher might have the copy as soon as possible, and he himself the money, he published in 1719: *The Life and Strange Surprizing Adventures of Robinson Crusoe, of York, Mariner: Who lived Eight and Twenty Years, all alone in an un-inhabited island on the Coast of America, near the Mouth of the Great River of Oroonoque; Having been cast on Shore by Shipwreck, wherein all the Men perished but himself.*

*With An Account how he was at last strangely de-
liver'd by Pyrates. Written by Himself. London.
Printed for W. Taylor at the Ship in Pater-Noster
Row. MDCCXIX.* In the entire world there have
been few books more famous.

For it has been singled out by the immense tribe of
children, a faithful tribe that does not easily forget
its gods. Defoe did not write it for little folk. The
little folk took it to themselves without ceremony.
They began by sifting it, until it was rid of those
heavy elements that its powerful current dragged
painfully along with it: those repeated sermons, those
first truths, namely, that human affairs are exposed
to changes and disasters; that the prosperity which
we abuse often becomes the source of our greatest misfortunes; that gratitude is not a virtue inherent in
human nature; that we must be satisfied with average
happiness for fear that Heaven condemn to an un-
favorable exchange whoever is not contented with
his lot. All excellent reflections, but so numerous and
overwhelming that they are capable of inciting
wrongdoing, if only to provide a little variety. And
they have also changed somewhat that puritan spirit
which tended to regard the adventures of Robinson
as a punishment from Heaven. If a son wants to be a
sailor against the wishes of his father, he will be sent
for twenty-eight years to a desert island and good
enough for him. As if tempests, shipwrecks, surprises
and battles could be considered punishment! They are,
on the contrary, magnificent rewards, reserved for
the daring and the strong. Now then, let men get to
work and cut down the story, leaving only its simplest
outlines; and let them, without hesitating, give the
children what they are seeking.

What stands out, first of all, is that credibility which Defoe has taken so much trouble to establish. Everything that Robinson says rings perfectly true. We could not doubt the word of such a meticulous, precise man. He reports the circumstances so well, adds details so abundantly that he lends to an imaginative story the force of reality. This is not just a hero of fiction, since he is seasick, drinks, eats, sleeps, is ill exactly as we might be, you and I. He furnishes accurate figures. We know that his voyage from Africa has brought him five pounds, nine ounces of gold dust, neither more nor less. If he is giving measurements, he is not mistaken by an inch nor by a line. Here is a man who knows how to add up, even in the most tragic circumstances. Robinson saw a whole band of savages, of cannibals, disembark on his island and make ready to devour a prisoner that they had brought with them. Having instilled courage into Man Friday, and equipped himself with an entire artillery, he approached, fired, killed or wounded several savages, freed the Spanish prisoner who had joined his benefactors in routing the cannibals. At present the business is ended; no business without good bookkeeping. So:

3 killed at our first shot from the tree.
2 killed at the next shot.
2 killed by Friday in the boat.
2 killed by ditto, of those at first wounded.
1 killed by ditto in the wood.
3 killed by the Spaniard.
4 killed, being found dropped here and there of their wounds, or killed by Friday in his chase of them.
4 escaped in the boat, whereof one wounded, if not dead.

---

21 in all.

This spirit of precision will never desert him. He will show us everything minutely: his animals, the plants in his garden, the walls of his hut, the ditches, the ramparts; his weapons, his pots and pans. Each event of his life takes on an almost historic aspect. We know all the detailed circumstances: the date, the year, the month, the day. This tone of scrupulous ingenuousness attracts young readers and gives them a sense of security. Free from uncertainty, they have only to give way to their pleasure. They no longer wonder if Defoe really made the voyages he tells about, which they can follow on the map at the end of the book; they believe it, word of honor. They scarcely notice the author's name; whoever wrote the adventures of Robinson Crusoe must be Crusoe himself. And no doubt they are wiser than men, who take for the author the poor creature of flesh and blood whom they enjoy watching as he lives, loves, suffers and sins. They forget that the true author is the one they will never see, the spirit that has embodied in the book his secret being, his real and inaccessible self.

What a queer and amazing fellow Robinson Crusoe is, with his long beard and pointed hat, his body covered with animal skins, armed both with a gun and a parasol, not to mention the parrot perched on his shoulder! And how busy he is! What a gift he has for holding the centre of the stage and stirring up our emotions! It is not only our curiosity and sympathy that he arouses; he actually wrings our hearts. Do you not see this print of a bare foot on the sand near the shore? Whose is it? Should he hope or tremble with fear? And the wicked cannibals who came on shore on purpose to roast their prisoners and to relish them shamelessly! And the sailors who mutinied, worse than the cannibals! These pages, worn by so many impatient and excited fingers, contain not only the adventures of Robinson Crusoe, they are heavy with the raptures, the fears, the dreams of young humanity. This magic book has released in thousands and thousands of hearts the passion for adventure, the same passion that stirred Sindbad the sailor, or Ulysses the Greek. Because of this magic quality, many a twelve-year-old adventurer has made believe that he left home, that he embarked intrepidly on sea voyages, that he was shipwrecked and that he lived forever after in a marvelous country!

Children have acted out this drama among themselves, in their garden, in their house; the strongest taking the role of Robinson Crusoe and the most faithful that of Friday. Sometimes they actually went away, escaping some fine morning without even looking back. They followed the high roads to find the harbor where they had been told that great ships stirred restlessly, ready to sail over the seas. The fact is they were yielding to the temptation of the unknown, of the uncertain, of the possible. The fact is that reading old Defoe awakened that nostalgia which makes all life one vast desire for migration. Like the domestic gander that Selma Lagerlöf tells about, they thought they heard the call of the wild geese, and rushed forth to join them way above the clouds in the blue sky. Less skeptical, less disillusioned than ourselves, perhaps children find, by contact with such pages, the strength and freshness of the primitive instincts of our race. Does the memory stir in them of times when our most remote ancestors were just beginning to wander over the earth? Does a voice from beyond call from such pages bidding the children to leave our island and drawing them towards kingdoms

57

which their earthly eyes will never be able to see?

Children like to destroy, we admit that; but they also like to build. Often, indeed, they destroy only to obtain material more to their taste. Building is one of their favorite games. They delight in building cardboard houses and wooden palaces, and nowadays automobiles, airplanes, and every kind of machine. What is there so surprising in their seizing upon *Robinson Crusoe,* if they find it to be a story of constructive ingenuity and energy? They also start out in life rather fearful. Like their great shipwrecked friend, they find themselves tossed onto an unknown land whose limits they will never know except by slow exploration. Like him, they are afraid of the darkness that falls. Night arrives and closes them in. Who knows if the sun will appear again tomorrow? They have everything to fear, beginning with hunger, with cold. Little by little they gain poise, are reassured, and begin to live on their own account. Just as Robinson does when he starts out to reconstruct his life.

He swims towards the boat that the waves are trying to destroy, builds a raft and brings back provisions. He overlooks nothing that can be of use to him today, tomorrow or in years to come. He salvages everything — clothes, tools, ropes, scrap iron; he takes even razors and forks from this blessed ship which provides him with all he has. " I really believe that if the weather had stayed fine, I would have brought the whole ship ashore, bit by bit—." This is only the beginning; soon he begins a second struggle. He wants not merely to exist but to be civilized, so he must have a house, a bed, a table and a fire — less because he esteems it pleasant to be sheltered and to have a comfortable bed than to demonstrate the triumph of his will over a destiny which meant to condemn him to live as a savage on a desert island.

He finds a way to control that fluid substance called Time, that slips so easily from our memory, by engraving, on wood, symbols of the days and months and years. He supports his days with a framework of habit. He will not become like the beasts that surround him. As he has saved his body so will he save his mind. He will force it to work, to inscribe itself on paper. His memory will be the safeguard for his ego. Perhaps the finest and most moving thing that Robinson did for us was to discover the enemy that is in every man's nature drawing him towards surrender, oblivion, and often hopelessness, and transforming this enemy into a helpful rival. He feels that what he did yesterday is never quite right or satisfying. The Robinson of tomorrow, cleverer, more skillful, will surpass the clumsy and tired Robinson who so far has produced nothing perfect. By engaging in struggle with this rival he reinvents progress.

Come typhoons, earthquakes, and floods which threaten to swallow him up, come sickness, fever, he knows now that he will be able to withstand them. He progresses from miracle to miracle. He recreates art in beautifying his furniture and his pottery, which are no longer just simple, useful objects. He recreates society. He has a dog, two prolific cats, kids, parrots that give him the illusion of hearing a human voice, and other tamed birds; and one fine day man himself appears in the form of the good savage, Friday. Friday's father, a European, and a Spaniard turn up also and collectivity is brought about by degrees.

My island was now peopled, and I thought myself very rich in subjects; and it was a merry reflection, which I frequently made, how like a king I looked. First of all, the whole country was my own mere property, so that I had an undoubted right of dominion. Secondly my people were perfectly subjected. I was absolute lord and law giver; they all owed their lives to me; and were ready to lay down their lives, if there had been occasion of it, for me. It was remarkable, too, we had but three subjects, and they were of three different religions. My man Friday was a Protestant, his father was a pagan and a cannibal, and the Spaniard was a Papist. However, I allowed liberty of conscience throughout my dominions. But this is by the way.

By the way, not entirely; in these words there are emotion and pride, for Robinson, the creator, admires his work and finds it beautiful.

Then there is Suzanne,[1] daughter of Jean; Suzanne, our contemporary, our friend, you who were shipwrecked on an island in the Pacific, who found life so pleasant and so easy (fine sand to sleep upon, fresh water for bathing, savory fruits to quench your thirst, the most gorgeous birds, the most opalescent fishes for your eyes to enjoy) that you did not take the trouble to do any work; what was the use? Suzanne, you made a bit of fun of Robinson, who, having had such a unique chance to free himself from the weight of civilization, had no other concern than to become again its prisoner, like a headstrong slave who returns to his chains. You are exquisite. We like you, Suzanne lost in the Pacific; we admire you for your charm, your impulsive animation, your brilliant way of clothing the paradox, and your keen wit! We should like to meet you, to hear the sound of your pretty voice, and through your eyes to see the world anew. For we are a little blasé, and you find a way of stimu-

[1] *Suzanne et le Pacifique,* by Jean Giraudoux.

lating and reviving our taste. May you be thanked and blessed for it.

But you will not enter the children's kingdom. They would never quite understand you and they would never exchange you for their good old Robinson Crusoe, who shows them, each and every one, how they can build the world all over again to suit themselves.

Gulliver's Travels

How did the children happen to get hold of Swift?

He was a man who, in all probability, would have frightened them stiff. Anyone could see at a glance that the gods, in bestowing their gifts, had meant him to be formidable. First of all, he was too lucid, being able to discern right off what is taking place in human hearts. Nothing is more dangerous than that. Whether it was a question of his enemies or of his friends or of himself, he was relentless. He burst all bubbles fiercely, even though they were iridescent. When he lost his temper, which often happened, he knew exactly why. On the other hand he was too sensitive. Blows stung him to the quick, retorts seemed unfair to him, and caresses irritated him so that he was always suffering. Such a condition eventually destroys sympathy. Friends willingly feel compassion for our ills, but we must try to arrange so they do not last too long. Swift was always suffering and was always a martyr. He suffered at Trinity College because he was poor, because his uncles paid for his studies, because he was superior to his masters, because matters that interested him were not exactly those that were on the curriculum or in the examinations. He suffered in William Temple's house for all sorts of reasons that would have made others perfectly happy — because he belonged in an exclusive society, because his duties as secretary permitted him to study and to work. He suffered when he received orders, when he threw himself into party struggles, when, as a Whig, he attacked the Tories, and as a Tory, the Whigs. He suffered when, beaten in politics, he regained his native Ireland, and was appointed Dean of Saint Patrick's at Dublin. Handsome, well set up, witty, learned, seeming to know everything intuitively, generous, always ready to champion the weak, he lacked, so it seemed, only two or three lesser qualities — patience, moderation. His talent, which amounted to genius, did not need them, but they would have changed the whole conduct of his life. He attracted and repelled at the same time, as men do when they carry within them the secret germs of a melancholy that develops as time goes on; and indeed, his life endured longer than his sanity.

No spirit was ever more ironical by nature, and that is a turn of mind that children do not understand. I imagine they would find distasteful his discreet proposition for preventing little Irish children from being a charge to their parents or to their country. It is a fact, says Swift, that Irish children are far too numerous. So numerous that even if they were trained early in life to beg and steal they would not be able to shift for themselves. So what can be done about it? They can't be sold as slaves, since they are scarcely of marketable value before they are twelve years old. "Now," continues Swift, "an American of my acquaintance, a man of excellent judgment, assured me that in London, a perfectly healthy young child, well fed, is, at the age of one year, a delicious and nourishing food, either boiled, roasted, steamed or baked; and I have no doubt that it could be equally well used in a fricassee or stew." " In short these children will be sold for the table of the rich after notifying the mother that she is to nurse them copiously during the last month, so they will be plump and fat." This cannibal humor must seem frightful to anyone not familiar with the realities of life.

When Swift published *Gulliver's Travels* in 1726, he allowed his talents full scope, displaying all his strength, using his abilities unreservedly. Men, his weak and foolish brothers, were imbeciles, in every sense of the word. Men were all puffed up with the stupidest kind of pride; he was going to reduce them all to their proper size. He was going to show them that power is a ridiculous invention, based on the stupidity of subjects and the cowardice of courtiers who are compelled to grovel before the king, actually licking the dust from the floor. He was going to show them that all religious and political quarrels are as futile as those which impel " big-enders " and " little-enders " to do away with themselves because they differ in opinion over the question of how a boiled egg should be cut open. He meant to prove to them, once and for all, that everything is relative. Strength is relative, because being a dwarf or a giant is simply a matter of comparison. Political systems are relative, because merely changing climates is enough to find a government absurd that one had formerly considered the peak of perfection. History is relative; it thinks it restores truth and does nothing but falsify everything it touches. As for philosophy, there is no kind of madness that has not been upheld by some philosopher. And as for science, oh! how grotesque those scholars are who reduce glass to ashes in order to make cannon-powder out of saltpeter, and those who try to build houses by beginning with the roof, and those who plough the earth with hogs, and those who replace silkworms with spiders! They are all mad, raving mad. Beliefs and customs are relative. Incest seems a crime to us, but it is just a simple deviation from our habits and manners that cannot be controlled by laws. Beauty is relative. How ugly the most beautiful of women seems as soon as our sight becomes one degree more penetrating! Her skin, which appeared to be soft and smooth as possible, is really old, spotted, ruined, frightful to see. Our loftiest dreams, our ideas of infinity and immortality are only added proofs of our madness. What more abominable fate could be ours than to become immortal, to resemble those Struldbrugs who prolong their decrepitude as though it were the most painful of burdens? Nothing is true, nothing is certain, except the infinite misery of the human condition.

Gulliver arrives in the land of horses and is put to shame by their kindness and wisdom. While there, he meets animals of an inferior species which, at first sight, disgust him. Long hair falls over their face and neck; their chest, hind and front paws are covered with thick hair; they have a beard on their chin as goats do. These animals sit or lie down or stand on their hind legs; they jump, leap and climb trees by means of their long, hooked claws. The females are a little smaller than the males; their face is hairless, but they have a thick head of brown, red, black or blond hair; their breasts hang between their two front paws. "Altogether," says Gulliver, " these animals seemed to me the ugliest and the most disgusting that I had ever seen, and no other species had made me feel so pronounced an antipathy."

These Yahoos, as they are called, these filthy beings justly condemned to eternal slavery, since they are incapable of raising themselves to a higher condition; these repulsive creatures, prey to the lowest vices — come now, there is no getting around it, we must face the fact that these are men. In vain Gulliver rebels, terrified; in vain he seeks differences in his own nature that set him apart from these monsters. There is no difference; he is like them — and indeed the Yahoos claim him as one of them. The noble horses, taking pity on him, expel him from their island to spare him the shame of appearing to be a member of this ignoble race.

That is how Swift speaks, with clear anger, calling on his exasperated sensitiveness to supply the most humiliating and offensive traits for us. Like Gulliver we try at first to rebel; we refuse to recognize ourselves in the caricature that he holds up before our eyes. But he pursues us, seizes us, forces us to admit the resemblance. We rouse from reading *Gulliver's Travels* with a feeling of having undergone an irremediable defeat. However, it is this book that the children have pointed out, saying: it belongs to us, it is ours. They do not want mawkish books, handed them with a smile, but they recognize as their own property what would seem to be the bitter food of men.

What do they care about the personality of Swift, his unhappy and passionate life? What do they care even about certain characters in the book that they do not, and cannot, understand? They are preoccupied with the book, and even in the book they select only what they like. Swift is ruled by his own impulses, and having begun with a smile, ends in fits of indignation and disgust. They remember only the smile. Once more, as in *Robinson Crusoe*, a band of workers offer their services to the children, simplifying, pruning, cutting across the rich fabric of the story. But no matter how clumsy they may be, allowing the mended places to show, daring even to add something of themselves, they can never do away entirely with the essential qualities of the book that children sense as diviners sense running water. For Swift's imagination gushes forth everywhere, all the more stupendous when it keeps its balance. It starts off with an impossible hypothesis, maintaining it with such perfect logic that it gives the impression of coherence and almost of truth.

Let us suppose that there exists a country whose inhabitants are no larger than your thumb, and that some fine day a normal man lands there by chance. There will follow a situation rich in surprises, but in surprises founded on dimension and arithmetic. How novel this tiny world appears! How frail those ropes are that the Lilliputians use to fasten Gulliver! How small that fleet is that he pulls up on the bank with one hand! And this little king that struts about, and this little queen in her palace, and those little ministers, and those little courtiers! And those barrels of wine and those cartloads of victuals that a seemingly enormous mouth gulped down at one swallow! But press the button, change the lens: the inverse hypothesis appears bringing with it many effects analogous and opposite to the first ones. There is new pleasure, new laughter, always with the same feeling of a sustained rule, of a constantly respected plausibility. On the soil of Brobdingnag the Lilliputians of a while ago have grown as tall as giants, while Gulliver's stature has remained the same. He has not changed and he seems very small at present; so small that they put him in a cage, make him walk on the queen's hand. A jealous dwarf throws him into a bowl of milk where he almost drowns. A mischievous monkey carries him away over the roofs. There is an admirable dexterity in this art of changing proportions. Let us recall, among many examples, the episode of the flies which are enlarged to the point of becoming odious and dangerous enemies.

I was frequently rallied by the queen upon account of my fearfulness; and she used to ask me whether the people of my country were as great cowards as myself. The occasion was this: the kingdom is much pestered with flies in summer; and these odious insects, each of them as big as a Dunstable lark, hardly gave me any rest while I sat at dinner, with their continual humming and buzzing about my ears. They would sometimes alight upon my victuals, leaving there their eggs and their excrement. Sometimes they would fix upon my nose or forehead, where they stung me to the quick, smelling very offensively, and I could easily trace that viscous matter, which, our naturalists tell us, enables those creatures to walk with their feet upwards upon a ceiling. I had much ado to defend myself against these detestable animals, and could not forbear starting when they came on my face. It was the common practice of the dwarf to catch a number of these insects in his hand, as schoolboys do among us, and let them out suddenly under my nose, on purpose to frighten me, and divert the queen. My remedy was to cut them in pieces with my knife as they flew in the air, wherein my dexterity was much admired.

The danger would lie in repetition, in an exact parallel between episodes, in monotony. Heaven be praised! Swift's imagination is inexhaustible; he invents scenes that no one has ever beheld — secret language, phantoms obedient to man, and even the temporary resurrection of the dead. After Brobdingnag, Laputa; after Laputa, the country of the Houyhnhnms. . . .

When the children made the irritable Dean of Saint Patrick's one of their benefactors, could they have understood his real personality? Could they have sensed all the force of love there was in him and felt that his rages were caused sometimes by the fact that he could not cherish, as he would have wished, a humanity not only imperfect, but incorrigible? That they were caused by a longing for tenderness eternally aroused but never gratified? Certainly children often have intuitions that place them in direct contact with great souls. Perhaps they are able to recognize, under a forbidding exterior, a sensitivity in despair. But let us not attribute too much perception to these fortunate young ones. What they like in Swift is a fanciful quality that surprises them, delights them and that, moreover, is always accessible to them. They like this miraculous imagination that leads straight to tales of voyages, to movement, to adventure, to the enchantment of the unknown, and that prolongs these voyages beyond the limits of the real, transforming them into an unending miracle, but that manages at the same time to be accurate and clear. They like its wild inventions that are not only comical but concrete.

Children recognize themselves in these multitudinous gambols. They themselves are dwarfs or giants. With their lords and masters, with the business, uproar and commotion of the world they are only dwarfs. With their toys, the cat purring before the hearth, the

68

pet dog whose ears they pull, they are imperious giants. Among hills and mountains, on the beaches, under the immensity of the sky, they are poor dwarfs, incapable of grasping anything. Among the flowers in the garden, bent over the swarms of ants, busy building their castles of sand, they are giants with unlimited power. In accompanying Gulliver from the diminutive palaces of Lilliput to the regions where there are houses higher than our forests, they recognize a miracle no longer disturbing to them since they are used to changing their own imagery, of reducing it or enlarging it, a hundred times a day.

They enjoy following Swift in his games, for he plays genuinely. He establishes rules and, once laid down, never breaks them but plays delightfully, profiting by all the latitude they allow him. His agile Gulliver runs and capers throughout his book, bumps his nose, picks himself up and sets off harder than ever to seek adventure. Swift places him in the most puzzling situation, pulls him out of it, launches him anew, has him flying about again. What fine sport! What facility! What an illusion of liberty there is in his perpetual motion! Any caprice, any device is permitted him. One might think that he is trying to see how far fancy can go within a given society. This fancy is so alive, so nimble, so glowing, so amusing that it forgets its own limits. It is still the best way we have found, if not of leaving our island, at least of forgetting sometimes that we are prisoners on it.

Don Quixote

The adventures of the Baron of Munchausen were not written for children. The story of the ingenious hidalgo Don Quixote de la Mancha, who became insane from reading so many books on chivalry, was not written for children. Cervantes had burdened his characters with too many feelings, too many ideas difficult to understand; the experience of a long life and the whole wisdom of a man who had read much and had associated even more with humanity. Cervantes conceived the idea of giving us twin souls in order to show by symbols how we are drawn at the same time upward towards the ideal and downward towards the material. Growing bolder as he went along he did not hesitate to suggest to us a Kindness always duped, always scoffed at, and yet victorious, since she arose stronger and surer of herself after each fall. Truths of that sort do not enter easily into young minds. Children need to test them fully before having faith in them. For Cervantes also said that we are sure neither of truth, nor of justice; that the evidence of our senses is not enough to make us believe that we see, and hear, and are in contact with reality; and that we all resemble, more or less, Don Quixote, who came out of a cavern of Montesinos knowing no longer himself if he had dreamed or if he had lived.

Cervantes enjoyed making a prolonged study of insanity, the most disturbing and the saddest of all human peculiarities, with its outbursts, its paroxysms, its melancholy. In short, he accumulated so many riches in his book that scholars have been busy for centuries hunting them out and are not sure yet of knowing them all. Without troubling themselves about the scholars, and leaving them to their task, the children have put the Cervantes that they have discovered and liked in their own library. They like the one who is gay, who rolls up adventures the length of the highways, who is not afraid of being lavish with cudgelings, always a joy to childish spectators; the one who depicted the yellow, thin, bony Don Quixote, perched on Rozinante, and the rubicund, plump Sancho, seated on his ass and lifting his elbow to quench his thirst with plenty of heady wine. They took possession immediately: " My book has had a great success," says Cervantes in the second part of *Don Quixote*; " everybody is reading it and soon there will no longer be a country where it is not translated. But the pages like it best of all. They fight over it in the Lords' antechamber. Scarcely has it ceased to be in one pair of hands, than another page takes it up again, and they burst into gales of laughter over it."

The pages' fresh outbursts of laughter, that is the sound that has accompanied the story of the ingenious hidalgo for more than three centuries. It is related that Philip III, seeing from his balcony a student who was reading in the street and who often broke off reading to go into shouts of laughter, cried out: " Either that student is crazy or he is reading the adventures of Don Quixote." The student was reading the adventures of Don Quixote as the King surmised. So it happened that Cervantes won over students and pages in Spain three centuries ago and since then he has won over all the children in the world.

The Children's World Today

Sure of their strength, children have continued to defend themselves. Refusing books that were offered them and choosing their favorites at will was a triumph, a real victory over their elders, at a time when elders were still the masters. Are they still the masters today? If observers, who enjoy watching the trend of the times, do not notice that one of the recent signs is the growing importance granted to children, they are indeed nearsighted. Perhaps old humanity is just a little tired of being authoritative. Perhaps it is becoming more tender or more just. The fact remains that today the children are our lords and masters.

They have won the right to have newspapers, like the grownups. Their young eyes, missing nothing that happens in the family, have seen the older people wait impatiently for the arrival of their favorite newspaper. They have seen them tear off the wrapper with an eager gesture, unfolding the huge sheet in front of them, absorbing, like demigods, all the wonders of the world. An admirable pastime — what is this I am saying? — a function, rather, that takes on the appearance of a rite, reflecting its importance on the officiant; a function desiring and deserving imitation; no more special privileges. So the children have been given their own special news sheets, eagerly looked for on Sundays and Thursdays. They have torn off the wrapper, unfolded the pages, read stories, commented on the pictures, become familiar with games and competitions; by becoming subscribers, entering a category superior to that of just ordinary readers, they have been elevated in their own esteem.

Before long they gained a foothold in the newspapers meant only for grownups; they invaded them. Newspapers have made room for the children just as they have had to make room for South America and the wireless. The serious man, informing himself about domestic and foreign politics, about traffic accidents and the market price of Rio Tinto, turns the page and beholds little drawings, little stories, little monologues. His place is no longer entirely his; the children have taken over a portion of his domain and installed a nursery in it. In his own youth he would never have dared dream of such usurpation. He is not too indignant, however, for he indulges in a secret weakness for these audacious little creatures that nothing can deter, and he lends them a kind of complicity.

After that the children wanted to have their own theatre. The time is not so far distant when it would have been termed scandalous if they had asked for anything but the circus, Punch and Judy, and occasionally a fairy spectacle. I remember, as a youth, I was never allowed to cross the sill of a theatre unless I had expressed an imperative urge to hear the classics. Without *Le Cid* and the baccalaureate, I would have had to wait until goodness knows what age. Even then I was not at ease on the red benches. I felt tolerated and not included. I was under surveillance of the graybeards. A theatre for children; after all, why not? So here they are now with their cleverly fashioned marionettes; their actors and their singers, their comedies and their operettas; their dancers and, upon my soul, their ballerinas. It is I, now, who feel barely tolerated in the little people's theatre, where I know myself to be too heavy, too big, too old.

They have their concerts. They have their cinemas. No longer are there domains reserved just for us men. When they cannot possibly penetrate where we are, they settle down opposite us and create rival institutions. They make their toys of our newest inventions. They no longer want railroads unless perfected even to catastrophe. They demand automobiles. They will have aeroplanes. Good-bye forever, dolls from Nu-

remberg. Farewell, farms, dairymaids with ruddy
cheeks, cowherds with pointed hats, too-green trees
and frizzly sheep. Farewell, rocking horses. No longer
is there anything new enough for the children. Consider little girls' clothes — their bright-colored frocks,
fitted coats, materials with ingenious patterns and
sophisticatedly childish styles. They even have their
own dressmakers and it is only by chance if little boys
do not have their own tailors. How could we go about
imposing books on them, through prestige or authority? Those who get mixed up with writing for
children are careful to ask them first of all what their
tastes and wishes are, and declare themselves to be
their very humble and obedient servants.

There fell into my hands an English book that
contains striking evidence of this rapid evolution.
Writing for Children[1] is the work of a specialist, a
technician, as they say today, who, having made his
reputation and fortune, wanted to expound the art
of writing for the use of beginners, his colleagues.
Beware, those of you who wish to enter this field, he
says to them. Do not fool yourselves into believing
that children are going to read any kind of stories,
and that all you have to do is to impose your taste on
them; that is a beautiful illusion. To succeed, start
out by believing just the contrary and be prepared
not to command but to obey: the children will be
your masters. The titles alone are extremely important,
for there are some that repel them right away, either
because they seem old-fashioned or deceptive. En-
title your story "John and Lucy at the Seashore,"
" How Little Violet Helped Her Mama," " How a

[1] Arthur Groom, *Writing for Children. A Manual of Juvenile
Fiction*. London. A. and C. Black. 1929.

74

Piano Is Made," "An Interesting Errand," "Marguerite at School," and you can be absolutely sure that the book will not be opened, or if it is, the reader has already made up his mind not to like it. Do not fail to start off with originality and liveliness; make use of dialogue in developing your story — that is what they want. Give them all the action you can, that goes almost without saying. Let your endings, while they satisfy their curiosity, leave something still open to wonder, so as not to close their horizon; for after they have finished the tale you have made up they will make up one of their own.

During the whole length of this book, for pages and pages, this experienced author lavishes advice in this fashion. Avoid wordiness, descriptions that only adults endure kindly; do not forget that almost before one round is ended your readers will be all set to ask you what happens next. They are indefatigable. Be brief, be nimble. Their capacity for emotion is considerable but they do not yet like sad emotions; after some vicissitudes, a happy ending is important. You may use as many plants and animals as you wish. Every candidate for success in literary material for children must visit a zoölogical garden at least several times a year. They have an innate sympathy for birds, fishes and insects; they commune with plants and flowers; sensing in themselves the same universal vitality. If you are relating adventures to them (sixty per cent at least of the books that bring in money and can be considered as good business are tales of adventure), remind yourselves that they must be thrilling; allow a certain realism in the ensemble and accuracy in the details. For instance, if you are telling about an automobile race, do not state that the winning car did its last six miles in six seconds. You, a writer, do not know, perhaps, the latest speed record of the automobile, but the children will know far more about it than you do. If you undertake to write a story about wireless telegraphy, pay attention to technical terms; do not fool yourselves, they are experts. Boy Scout material is an excellent mine for authors provided they do not repeat a good deed which the children have already heard a hundred times: how the scout attracted the attention of the mad bull that was charging a little girl, or how he saved the farmer about to perish in his blazing barn. In short, future writers of best-sellers, you who want to succeed in this field, as others do in the bandit or ghost-story market, you must keep in mind a certain number of exact rules and one principle: perhaps formerly children accepted without protest the books put in their hands, however boring they were; in those days they were easier to please, or better brought up; but today, to please them, you must first submit to their demands.

And genius, that touch of genius, without which a lasting work could not be composed, either for little or big folk? How to acquire it? The manual does not say; it did not think of that.

The fact remains that a change has come about in our old world. What will happen if, instead of multiplying rapidly as in the past, children become a species more and more rare and more and more precious? " Talk all you want to," the father of a family says to me, " about the time when children used to be oppressed by men; I am telling you that the time will come when men will be oppressed by the children."

III

SUPERIORITY OF THE NORTH
OVER THE SOUTH

The Southern Lack of Children's Books

I WOULD grant, without argument, that the South is superior in everything with the exception of one thing. In the matter of literature for children the North surpasses the South by a large margin.

Why?

Spain, to start off with, is singularly lacking in books for children. What magnificent profusion abounds in a Lope de Vega, a Calderon! What constantly original strength has prevailed, from the picaresque novel to the sublime effusions of Saint Theresa! Spain has a passion for color, a sense of mystery, an innate gift of poetry. She is brimful of imagination. As she is not bothered either by a prejudice for styles, or worry about rules, her taste remains perfectly free and her soul is close to primitive spontaneity. But she does not possess any literature for children. Yesterday her sons and daughters read Defoe, Jules Verne or Salgari. Today they read tales of travels and novels of adventure that come from North America. Yesterday they borrowed *Don Quixote* and today they take the simple, moving scenes from the most delicate of poets, the *Platero y yo* of Juan Ramon Jiménez. " My book went forth and met the children," says the author; and he was happy over it, for he agrees with Novalis that wherever there are children a golden age exists, a fortunate island where it is so good to live that no one ever wants to leave it . . . but that is another matter. There is no Spanish author who has written especially for his young brothers and who in doing so has expressed himself with genius.

Italy has its *ninne-nanne* — sweet songs made to accompany the rocking of the cradle; it has its rounds, its games to sing, its melodies. It has books in its possession that interpret vigorously the spirit of the race, as we shall see presently. It can claim several writers who have become popular in the children's realm. But when everything has been gathered in, the harvest remains poor in comparison with its other riches which are so superb. Whenever a critic there is hard up for copy, he wonders why Italian literature is not popular; and he sets forth the reasons, repeating them again and again, adding new ones *ad libitum*. Is it because of the aristocratic character of their national genius? Or its lengthy tradition of learned accomplishment? Or its taste for delicate, chiseled work? Or a partiality for form? The fact still remains that a literature for children has been strangely late in coming about in Italy and that its two masterpieces, *Pinocchio* and *Cuore,* waited centuries to make themselves known; they date only from the Risorgimento.

Could we think of a Dante, a Petrarch, a Boccaccio, a Machiavelli, an Ariosto or a Tasso or, in more recent times, a D'Annunzio or a Carducci absorbed in studying the child's soul? What interests them is to exalt man, to push his faculties for æsthetic enjoyment or for conquests by violence to the extreme limits of the possible. Even a Manzoni, the most serenely human of all authors, bending the most tenderly over lives of the humble, has left no tale for little children.

The case of France is more complicated. France is a country where the Pros and Cons face each other readily. It boasts, quite naturally, of possessing Perrault. During the entire end of the seventeenth century it played with fairy tales. We have called attention to writers in decline today, formerly celebrated and translated throughout the world — Madame de Genlis, Berquin. If one wanted to make a complete list it would be long. We should have to evoke Nodier, Paul de Musset, George Sand and many others up to the time of our contemporaries. Today many distinguished women and talented authors are listening to little children and repaying their confidences with fine, subtle, colorful tales.

Without claiming first rank, at least we French are not in the rear. But our race is not exclusively Latin; and even with us the North puts in its claim. Erckmann-Chatrian were rather of the North than the South. Jules Verne, who knew how to interpret the instinct for invention and discovery at the heart of the children of men and has never ceased to be a favorite author with boys, knew no more ardent sun than that of Amiens. Madame de Ségur has become ours by right of preference and affection — and so it goes.

We French admire particularly works which interpret the full consciousness of the ego; and if we go off seeking obscure riches it is in order to analyze and clarify them. We do not like confusion and vagueness. Because of our love of speech we scorned, up to the time of Rimbaud, literature not organized on a logical plan, not expressed by an oratorical cadence. Very rarely do we give full flight to our dreams. As soon as pure imagination gets loose we put a bridle on it. We bring it back towards more moderate slopes, our natural region. So for all these reasons, our art turns away a little from the primitive, which it confuses with the puerile. I know many Frenchmen who cannot hear children's literature spoken of without shrugging their shoulders; and this adjective alone, applied to literature, " *enfantin,*" lowers its value in their minds. Books for children are no more interesting to them than dolls or puppets, and perhaps a little less. These serious people would blush to be seen fingering the pages of a *Bibliothèque Bleue* or *Rose,* as if they had been caught spinning a top, or exercising their venerable limbs running after a hoop.

The Nursery Rhymes of England

Now go towards the north, cross the Channel and mingle for a while with the English. You will see that England claims, even for her children, quite justly, that respect for the individual which is one of the dogmas of her moral life. She does not wait for them to become adults before granting them that right to liberty which she has passionately defended all through her history. Her sons can barely lisp before she gives them a golden book.

How strange those nursery rhymes appear to Latin minds! They seem to spring from the hidden depths of the nation's soul! The lullabies of Latin countries give only a remote and feeble idea of them. The English nursery rhymes are often only music, singing vowels, repetitions of sound, simple cadences stressed, full and sonorous rhymes. They are not unconscious of the fact that by placing rhythm at the beginning of life they are conforming to the general order of the universe. They have a harmony all their own that is strange, mocking, and tender. The sense is of less importance than the sound. Sometimes they recall the great events in a child's life — Humpty Dumpty who climbed up the wall and fell down again; Jack Horner who pulls a plum from his pudding and is proud of his performance, the cake that the baker has cooked, already devoured by eager eyes; slight scenes, slight stories, ending with an amusing and lively touch. Or they call in the animals: the mouse that runs up the clock, the geese in the farmyard, the gray pony.

> Pussy-cat, pussy-cat, where have you been?
> I've been up to London to look at the queen . . .
>
> I had a little hen, the prettiest ever seen;
> She washed me the dishes, and kept the house clean.

The word " little " occurs often, as is natural for little people: Little Betty Blue, Little Polly Flinders, Little Tommy Tucker; and that little husband who was no bigger than a thumb. Suddenly we find bits of history, epic and legend, strangely simplified, fallen from man's kingdom into that of children, gathered up and interpreted by them; great names taken from their majestic background and used in a spirit of fun, childlike shadows of those who bore them. There are dream people who have found their way into a jingle: the man in the moon, the good woman who climbed higher than the moon to sweep the cobwebs out of the sky. From time to time we seem to hear a mother's voice pouring out the love she bears her child; little matter the words she utters, their caress and their vibration alone are important. As the song moves towards its end, all meaning is done away with, and the last lines end in a kiss. And the whimsical is there also, the abrupt distortion that provokes laughter, the unexpected turn, the cock-and-bull story, rhymes that become ludicrous by their surprising association, the syllables that seem to caper about in foolish repetition. Silver-toned rattles, tinkling bells, sonorous rings, they fill the child's room with joyous sound; and like the fine lady who rode a fine horse, with rings on her fingers and bells on her toes, they make music wherever they go:

> Ride a cock-horse to Banbury Cross,
> To see an old lady upon a white horse,
> Rings on her fingers, and bells on her toes,
> And so she makes music wherever she goes.

Strange assembly, that escapes the laws of logic and is scarcely more than pure imagination. Imagination not unbridled, but which has not yet known the bridle. Caprice not unchained, but unaware of any chain. The happiness of a simple heart that peoples the world with its creations, asking of them only a flash of gaiety, of pleasure. At night, so the tales tell us, the people in the nursery rhymes come out of the book where old Mother Goose keeps them shut up during the day; they fraternize. King and Queen of

Hearts, do you forgive the Knave of Hearts who stole the tarts?

> The Queen of Hearts,
> She made some tarts,
> All on a summer's day;
> The Knave of Hearts
> He stole those tarts
> And took them clean away.

Little Miss Muffet, are you still afraid of the big spider that came and sat down beside you? Do you continue to fight for the possession of the crown, you, the unicorn, and you, the lion? And you, the fat man, the man of Bombay, have you found your pipe that a bird had stolen from you? And you, Mother Hubbard's dog, do you feel obliged to keep up your nonsense or do you rest a little at night?

> Old Mother Hubbard
>   Went to the cupboard
> To get her poor dog a bone;
> But when she came there
> The cupboard was bare,
>   And so the poor dog had none.

> She went to the baker's
>   To buy him some bread,
> But when she came back
>   The poor dog was dead.

> * * * *

> She went to the tavern
>   For white wine and red,
> But when she came back
>   The dog stood on his head.

> * * * *

She went to the hosier's
   To buy him some hose,
But when she came back
   He was dress'd in his clothes.

The dame made a curtsey,
   The dog made a bow;
The dame said, "Your servant,"
   The dog said, " Bow, wow."

You are all of you oddities. Far from behaving as
actors who give a performance for the pleasure of
others, your first concern is to have a delightful time
yourselves. You have humor, charm, freshness; but
what makes you inimitable is that all of you have at
heart a dash of poetry.

For if, by an act of impiety, we should try to put
these nursery rhymes into prose, we would no longer
have anything but ashes left from a fire. The magic
quality of cadence, of rhyme, is seen here at its best.
If they are not related to prayer through spiritual
aspiration, which is its highest form, they recall at
least incantation, which is its first form. They are
the poetry exactly suited to childhood, pictures in
rhyme. The little English children learn them by
heart. They say them, they sing them, they dance
them. They will never entirely forget them after they
are grown up. They will spring up from the lower
planes of consciousness where they have been tossed
aside by practical matters, by useful and useless
knowledge acquired throughout the days. They will
return of themselves to the lips, and we shall hear
serious men, suddenly mindful of the past, recite
them again with a smile. They are part of tradition,
like the Christmas tree. They provide a mutual bond

among Englishmen scattered throughout the Empire and who meet by chance at Melbourne, at Calcutta. Those who have not learned the nursery rhymes could not understand each other fully. Those who recited them when they were in short clothes are united by a brotherly sentiment.

But with the Latins, and especially with the French, poetry remains a luxury not to be dealt with before a certain age. It is a rational pleasure that must be clearly understood. The idea of a fascination where there is nothing to understand, just fantasy, resonance and rhyme, seems lunacy to them. Consequently no poetry was provided for the children unless they were assigned some mournfully puerile verses written, perhaps, by experienced adults, or some of La Fontaine's *Fables* that were much too difficult for them as we well know. And let them be satisfied with that until they are old enough to learn to compose Alexandrines.

As her children advance in age, old England keeps in touch with them. She knows how to be rigorously egoist, but she holds inexhaustible tenderness in reserve for those she loves. She develops their favorite media, poetry and fiction as well as adventure and sport, and makes even school life a profitable theme. In one of her classics, *Tom Brown's School Days*, we find a sentence borrowed from the Rugby *Journal* that has much to say about the rights of children in England: "If, on the one hand, we must remember that we are children, and children at school, we must keep in mind, on the other hand, that we form a complete social body, a society in which we must not only learn, but act and live." Conscious of this pride and independence, she lends to this usually difficult theme a half-lyrical tone that even strangers find sympathetic. She asks her designers and painters to create pleasing pictures for young eyes; and the artists, far from feeling themselves lowered by this appeal, create an original genre of great merit. She asks her writers to make their talent flexible, to refresh without debasing it. She leads them towards the Fountain of Youth. *When We Were Very Young,* A. A. Milne makes the title of one of his famous books, illustrated by E. H. Shepard; and indeed he speaks in it as he did during his early youth; not as though he were recalling it with an effort but as though he were going back to it. Without explanations and dull analysis he intuitively shares the pleasures and sorrows, the always tempestuous emotions of a young growing soul. Like little Billy Moon, to whom the book is dedicated, he is afraid that his mother might be crushed by an automobile if she ventures out without him. He has four friends, the elephant and the lion in the Zoo, a goat and a snail. He is very careful to keep from walking on the lines in the pavements, lest the bears that hide in the basements of London houses might pounce out suddenly. Publications of every kind multiply, the *Annuals,* the *Monthlies,* and the *Weekly Magazines,* all bearers of joy, by the year, the month, the week. Such abundance and such quality! Such tender care and affection given to childhood!

Children's Books in the United States

You may talk about the invasion of machinery in North America, where you feel that the development of the soul is being confused with material progress; where you deplore the tendency towards uniformity, the disappearance of individual initiative; where you denounce the dangers of a life that has only standardized work for occupation and only sports and the cinema for relaxation. But do not overlook the facts that can be put just as fairly on the other side of the scales. And, because it concerns us here, do not overlook the vigorous spirit that persists wherever the sympathetic question of childhood is brought up. What wonderful efforts have been made to safeguard it, to nourish its spirit, to provide the choicest foods for its curiosity! Explorers set forth from America to all the countries of the world to bring back new story material. Artists, designers, engravers, painters from all the countries in the world arrive in America, invited to decorate the pages of children's books. The élite of the country, that long-suffering élite which rebels against any diminution of the spirit, surrounds the coming generation with a solicitude probably unequaled anywhere as a treasury of hope.

Among the many sentiments that have stood the test of time and mingling of races, the men on the *Mayflower* took over with them the respect and love for childhood, and this respect and love have borne fruit in the new soil. Do many people know how many books are printed in the United States, for the use of children? In 1919, twelve million; in 1925, twenty-five million, two hundred thousand; in 1927, thirty-one million. In 1919 appeared four hundred and thirty-three new works intended for young people; in 1929, nine hundred and thirty-one. Every bookshop of importance has a juvenile department with its own employees and organization that functions alongside the large one. I have before my eyes a splendid volume, *Realms of Gold in Children's Books.*

Presented with taste, illustrated, it contains in eight hundred pages the notice, and sometimes the analysis, of all the books in the English Language, original or translated, that a child could wish for. What publishing house, what bookshop, in our country, would do as much for him? Queer country where they do not seek to make sordid economies in everything, and especially in books. Where they do not disdain to make works cheaply, but where they do not think either that cheapness is necessarily and always the last word in perfection; where they will permit neither poor paper nor worn-out type, nor faded ink, nor insufficient binding, nor misprints shamefully displayed. Where they seek to arouse not only the love but the habit of beauty from early childhood.

Here is an innovation that does honor to the sensibility of a people, and it is an American innovation: the libraries reserved for children. Those light and gay rooms, decorated with flowers and suitable furniture; those rooms where children feel perfectly at ease, free to come and go; to hunt for a book in the catalogue, to find it on the shelves, to carry it to their armchair, and to plunge into the reading of it. They are better than a drawing room or a club. They are a home. And how many children, in these huge cities without tenderness, have none other one but that! Outside, the rhythm of life tells of fever. A great human stream roars by. Millions and millions of men, so crowded against each other that space is lacking and houses fuse together towards the sky, keep in motion those gigantic factories called New York or Chicago. Everybody works hard, everyone is breathless until the evening signal sends him back to his suburb, where even his leisure will still be mechanical. Meanwhile, it is a different leisure that delights the children in those peaceful libraries peopled with books. There, where they feel so much at home, they are cultivating those qualities of spirit and soul which alone will be able later to solve the meaning of all this unbridled activity that must be controlled or condemned.

All respect is shown to the child. He is not asked if he is rich or poor, Catholic, Presbyterian or Quaker. He has complete freedom. From the hundreds or thousands of books within reach of his hand, he takes the one that pleases him. He may remain ten minutes or several hours. In Europe, too many librarians behave as though it was their business to protect their own work or sleep *against* readers; as if the intruders who dare to enter their abode were their personal enemies. You bother them: they are not there to be useful to you. You are there to endure their bad humor. Besides, the book that you ask for is being bound, or lent, or lost . . . go away. In the United States, I never asked for a book without being made to feel that I was rendering a service to the person who waited on me. And young visitors know very well that they will find peace and joy in their libraries.

Some day when your stroll leads you towards the old quarter that surrounds the Church of Saint Séverin in Paris, go and see the library that Americans have organized for the little French children and for the foreigners that live in this locality — Orientals, Russians, Poles. Nearly all the nations are represented in this confusion of ugly houses, in these narrow streets that recall the time when Villon frequented their hovels and taverns. The street has kept its savory name: Boutebrie Street. Enter. Everything seems to smile at you; the young women who manage it, the books dressed in becoming colors, and not only those crowded together on the shelves, but the fine books, wide open, that graciously allow you to see their drawings, their engravings; the flowers, the trees in the court which extends beyond the large room; and the children. There enters a well-behaved boy who comes here to write out a lesson impossible for him to do at home. In a moment you see him plunged into tales of travel, into geography books. Two little girls come in and set about consulting the list with a fine air of gravity. Enters a strapping fellow who would be unbearable right away, that is plain to see, if he was at grammar or high school. But here he does not have to combat anyone. He is someone. He is at home; not a passing guest but master of the house. If he tore any pages he would be committing a crime. If he disturbed the peace he would lose his self-respect. He made a promise with all the others when, in his big handwriting, he wrote in the register: " In writing my name in this book, I become a member of *L'Heure Joyeuse*, and promise to take care of the books and to help the librarian make our Library pleasant and useful to all." The Joyful Hour is not only the one spent in reading, there is also the story hour. Every Thursday, from October to May, at half past four, a group of small listeners settles down around a storyteller, and it is better than the cinema.

A hundred readers frequent the Library every day. Each month a general assembly is held which studies events that happen as the days go by. The assembly elects two heads, a boy and a girl, who are responsible for the appearance of the room, who admit the new-comers and sometimes manage the lending library.

What has become of you, library of my childhood? It was in a northern town where they were busier weaving cloth than cultivating their spirit. The librarian was an old man, gouty and grumpy, who was in despair when asked for a book so high up that he was forced to climb a ladder. That library was solitary and sad. It was the kingdom of the dead. What is more, no one could enter it except as a very special favor; libraries are not made for children. That is not what they think on Boutebrie Street.

" It is not a scholastic library, one of those cupboards locked with a key, discreetly hung on the wall of a classroom, and where some twenty volumes represent the whole stock speedily exhausted by the pupils. Nor is it one of those so-called popular libraries too often relegated, even in the large cities, to the dark rear of a shop where the volumes, uniformly bound in sad black cloth, dirty and full of germs, are distributed at evening by an employee christened librarian, who would be mightily astonished if told that he has a pedagogic function, and that he should be able to advise his readers. The library for children, according to the definition which has been given to it in America, is a home rather than a school." In these excellent terms Charles Schmidt, a general inspector of libraries, expresses himself; and he shows us how the example and the initiative of the United States are winning over, little by little, France and Europe.

Emulation is ardently encouraged, so that new authors may be born to rank with the classics of childhood. There are prizes, rewards. Each year a medal is awarded to the writer who has produced the best book, a medal which bears the name of the philanthropic bookseller of St. Paul's Churchyard,

John Newbery. Continuous effort is made by the most powerful associations of booksellers and educators. There are schools, courses for the training of children's librarians; foundations and scholarships which enable them to go and study what is useful and new in the countries of their choice; lending libraries, country libraries, sending of books by mail to distant villages; bookmobiles; intensive production, not made arrogant by success, but always seeking something better. All this I have seen in the United States.

Hans Christian Andersen

Supposing that, by some stretch of imagination, we were called upon to choose the very prince of all story writers for children, my vote would go, not to a Latin, but to Hans Christian Andersen.

Andersen was born on April 7, 1805, at Odense in Denmark, a fishing village by the gray waves of the Baltic. His father was a cobbler, so poor that he made his own wedding bed from the remains of an old bier. His mother sang to him the old Danish songs, and both parents imbued him with a spirit of the soil which nothing was ever to change. When he was fourteen years old, Copenhagen welcomed him, and if ever a town watched tenderly over an adopted son, appreciating him and divining the genius which stirred obscurely in his soul, this was the town. The tailor's trade did not suit him; he wanted to become a dancer, a singer, an actor, and he found patrons who helped and supported him, sent him to school. An awkward lad, over-tall, very thin, with big nose, hands and feet, he was ridiculous among his smaller classmates as a frightened swan among a flock of ducks. He was sent to the university, obtained a traveling scholarship, and finally, in 1839, after writing many essays, stories, poems and novels, his first volume of children's tales brought joy to all his countrymen.

I have made the pilgrimage. I have found his spirit alive. The old lady who received me, thin and aged, moved her hands as though to call him and to gather together the fragments of the past. She smiled at him through the darkness. " He used to sit in this corner near the window, and each time he wrote a new tale, he came to tell it to us, the children. I was his little Louise. For us he used to cut out of paper with scissors kings and queens, ladies in crinoline, clowns, landscapes, arabesques. How large his hands seemed to us! They were skilful, those large and heavy hands, and his scissors never erred. Look at his portrait, that is his writing you see at the bottom: ' Life is the most beautiful of adventures.' Look at these fans, on each fold the autograph of a famous man, it was his own idea. This screen made during an illness; he took pictures from the papers, from magazines and pasted them so each was a unit, one fold of the screen for each country; here is France. . . . "

In the large salon with the white panels, whose windows look out on the flower market, on the fish market, on the château, on the heart of Copenhagen, nothing is changed. Andersen could knock on the door, his high hat on his head, carrying in his hand his inseparable umbrella; he could take his familiar place again and begin the story of the nightingale or of the brave tin soldier. Going through the streets where he wandered, staring at the old houses he loved, crossing the thresholds he crossed, accompanying him

93

step by step, we follow one of the most beautiful existences that any man on earth has lived. It begins with extreme poverty, it knows desperate and hopeless effort, it is filled with lovely and exotic pictures, with passionate and always disappointed love affairs, with great, consoling friendships. It ends in glory and is crowned with immortality.

He is unexcelled because, within the slender framework of his tales, he brings in all the pageantry of the universe. It is never too much for children. You will find there not only Copenhagen and its brick houses, and its great reddish roofs and copper domes, and the golden cross of Notre-Dame that reflects the sun; Denmark with its marshes, its woods, its willows bent by the wind, its ever-present sea; Scandinavia, Iceland, snowy and frozen, but you will also find Germany, Switzerland, Spain flooded with sunshine, Portugal, Milan, Venice, Florence and Rome, Paris, city of the fine arts, city of revolutions. You will find there Egypt, Persia, China, the ocean to its very depths where the mermaids live; the sky where floats the whiteness of great wild swans.

It is a marvelous picture book that the moon makes in relating what she saw in the mountains, over the lakes, through the windows of human dwellings, in every place where her blue and melancholy light softly steals, plays and vanishes. If the present is not enough, evoke the past — Pompeian villas or the barbaric palaces of the Vikings. If reality is not enough, see magic scenes that the fairies build. If your eyes are not surfeited by nature's countless spectacles, close them; in your dreams will appear the luminous spirit of the truth, variable, ever changing, and more beautiful than the beauties of the waking day.

In these feasts of imagination, others will perhaps be capable of equalling him, but there are values he has revealed that are his very own sumptuous gift to children; enchanted scenes they will find only in him, the memory of which will charm them forever. Snow — Latin children hardly know it. Those at Naples or Granada never see it except from afar, way up high on the mountains. Scarcely does it appear before the eyes of small Parisians when it is changed into soot and mud. And where else would they get such another vision of icy vastness? Andersen opened up to them the fairylike domains of frost.

What strange beauty in his depiction of the glacial ocean where icebergs float like sea-faring monsters! What a sight is revealed to the fifth mermaid sister who becomes familiar with the world seen on the winter sea!

Now came the turn of the fifth sister. Her birthday, it happened, was in winter, and so she saw what the others had not seen on their first visit. The sea was all green to look at, and round about there floated large icebergs, every one looking like a pearl, she said, and yet they were far bigger than the church towers that men built. They showed themselves in the strangest shapes and were like diamonds.

Winter over the town, placing curtains on the window panes that the children must clear away with their breath if they wish to see the house opposite. Winter that turns the fingers blue, that numbs the limbs of the little match-seller, that causes Knud, the lover, to pass from his dream into eternal sleep. Winter that makes the snow man grow proud, thinking that his mere glance suffices to make the sun hurry down behind the horizon. Winter on the dunes, that the tempest seems to push back still further inland, making waves of sand that cover up the village chapels. The Winter King, as he rules in Lapland, almost burying animals and men, lord of stark immensity. These are some of the spectacles that Andersen offers and lavishes on children.

Thanks to him, we have seen through our own eyes the Snow Queen all in ice, her eyes shining like bright stars. With little Kay, we fastened our sledge to her white one. She let us sit beside her. We glided over the soft surface and were lifted into the air. We passed over forests and lakes, land and seas. Below us blew a glacial wind, wolves howled, snow sparkled. Above black crows were flying, cawing. And away up above shone the moon, large and bright. Thus we arrived at the Queen's Palace.

The walls of the Palace were made of drifting snow, and the windows and doors of biting winds. There were more than a hundred halls, shaped by the drifting of the snow. The largest of them stretched out for many miles, and all were lit up by the bright Northern Lights. These halls were tremendous — so empty, so icy-cold, so dazzling. There was never any gaiety here, not even the smallest dance for the bears, at which the storm winds could make the music, and the polar bears walk on their hind legs and show off their good manners. There was never a party where they played at muzzle-slapping and paw-clapping, and never did the white fox-girls forgather to enjoy a bit of gossip over their coffee. Empty, vast, and icy-cold were the Snow Queen's halls. The Northern Lights glowed at such regular intervals that one could reckon exactly when they would be at their highest and lowest. In the midst of the immense empty snow hall was a frozen lake, cracked into a thousand pieces, and each piece so resembled all the others that it looked like a real work of art. When at home the Snow

Queen sat in the very center, and then she said she was sitting on the "Mirror of Reason," which according to her was the only one that counted in this world.[1]

Fortunate indeed if in all this snow, our heart was not frozen as happened to little Kay:

Little Kay was quite blue with the cold, indeed almost black, and his heart was practically a lump of ice. But he was not aware of it, because the Snow Queen had kissed away the icy chill. He was busy fitting together a few flat sharp-edged pieces of ice, and trying to shape them into some kind of pattern, for he wanted to make something out of them, just as we do when we make Chinese puzzles with little squares of wood. Kay was arranging patterns, and most intricate ones, in that game known as the "Puzzle of Ice-cold Reason." To him these figures appeared very remarkable and of the greatest importance because of the chip of glass in his eye. He put together patterns to form a written word, but he could never manage to spell out the one word he had in his mind — the word "Eternity."[1]

We should be fortunate indeed if, as in the tale, some little Gerda followed us to the end of the world, to the very palace of the Snow Queen, and with her warm tears made the block of ice melt. Fortunate if, through love, she permitted us to solve the puzzle and to recover the lost word.

Andersen is unique in his capacity for entering into the very soul of beings and of things.

That animals have an intelligible language, Andersen and children know better than anyone. When the cat says to little Rudy: "Come out on the roof; put one paw here, another a little higher; come on, hoist yourself up; see how I do it, nothing is easier," little

[1] As translated from the Danish by Paul Leyssac in *It's Perfectly True and Other Stories*. Harcourt, 1938.

Rudy understands perfectly. And the dog that, not satisfied with barking, expresses himself also with his eyes, his tail, and his whole body speaks a language that seems quite natural to the child. That plants talk is taken for granted also. After all, why should Mother Elder and Father Willow not exchange confidences like everybody else? Leaves are very talkative; they murmur for no reason at all.

But what is rarer and finer is to see objects become animated and to hear their voices. Not only the toys, not only the porcelain dancer on the mantelpiece so full of airs and graces, not only the grotesque Chinese figure on the console who shakes his head when looking at you. This innumerable folk, that the indifferent call "things," stirs, moves, speaks and fills the air with its complaints or its songs. Everything is alive: the ray of sunshine that dances through the window, the branch of apple tree in its spring frock, the salon furniture, the gardener's tools, the kitchen utensils, the pail, the broom, the basket, the plates and even the matches, although they are a bit stiff. Of all the objects that you can imagine, there is not one that does not want to chat with its neighbors and make merry. At night, you believe there is no longer any life. On the contrary, it is the moment when silent ones feel free to speak; when the motionless ones feel their limbs itching and gambol about gaily. The arithmetic problem fidgets about on its slate, the letters grow restless in the copy book and complain at having been badly traced.

When one is a child, and can hardly talk, one understands perfectly the language of the hens and ducks, dogs and cats. They speak to us as distinctly as father and mother. At that age we even hear grandfather's cane whinny; it has become our horse, and we see a head on it, legs and a tail. But once grown up this faculty is lost. However, there are children who keep it longer than others; we say of them that they remain big simpletons. . . .

Big simpletons or geniuses. On this latter count, let us thank Heaven that Andersen remained a child.

If others shrivel up everything they touch by analyzing and dissecting, Andersen, on the contrary, animates and vivifies. On the summit of mountains, on the highest peaks, he is hypnotized by Vertigo who tries to make him totter and fall headlong into the abyss. In the depths of the crevices lives the Queen of the glaciers. She is asking for her victims, and you hear her voice. Andersen is never alone. He is surrounded by a multitude of little lives, by countless beings who observe and watch him. He is only one of them, perhaps a little better endowed, in the vast comedy in which thousands of actors take part. All the others, the oak, the house, the butterfly, the wave, the stick of wood, the gravestone, rejoice or suffer with him. Hallucination that is perhaps not altogether voluntary nor altogether false, if it does nothing more than translate the mystery of being and the constant vibration of things.

How conscious we are in all this of the powerful imagination of the North, instinct with sensitiveness! How different it is from the imagination of the South which etches everything sharply under the direct brilliance of the sun! Beneath this sky laden with mists, where the light remains timid and gray even on the fairest days, we grasp the significance of doubts and confusions. There the sharpness of a too clear vision will not belie the man who sees grimacing faces in the tree roots, who peoples the sea with phantoms delicately traced on its grayish expanse. When he expresses himself, as the law of our nature demands, he does so with less pride and authority. He is never entirely sure that the tricks of his imagination are really nothing more than imagination. He likes to pretend that the questions, the appeals which he attributes to the universe, come actually from the universe and not from himself. Uncertain of himself, he respects the essential character of things as though by raising them to his own sphere he were finding friends on his lonely and colorless horizon. Feeling deference for every living thing, he promotes animals to his own level. Why should they not have the right to be themselves? The storks, in appearance all alike, clothed in white and black and wearing red stockings, why should they not have their own personality? The birds of woods or field, why should they not have different characters as they have different feathers?

And, by a transition from the external to the hidden life, why should we not try to discover the individual soul of each object? If it is nothing but a diversion, at least it is generous and merciful. That old lantern which has shared existence with humans, which was useful to them for keeping off the dangers of the night, seems to have will power. It persists in struggling against the wind, against the rain. It seems to have intelligence, for it is interested in the adventures of the passers-by to whom it lends its reflection. And a sensibility, for it suffers when it sees the misfortunes around it. Its ambition is to endure, to persist in its being. It has a horror of annihilation. And so on, continuing the dream, multiplying it to infinity. The starched collar is proud of its rigid splendor. The teapot looks disgusted and will sing only when it is warm. And the silver shilling, if we tell it that it is only a counterfeit piece, shivers with indignation.

When we finish reading the *Tales* we are not entirely the same as we were when we began them. We would gladly become, as Rimbaud says, *un opéra fabuleux*. The wheat that bends, what emotion makes it tremble? Where do the white clouds go that are passing over us? Do they go in light attire to some celestial festival in the palace of Prince Azur?

But of all Andersen's claims to supremacy, the finest and noblest claim is the wisdom inherent in his tales, their inner life. There is much sorrow in the world, Andersen believes. The woman you love does not love you. She says she would like to be your sister. It is not the same thing. She becomes a great singer, or goes abroad, or marries someone else. She forgets you. There is also death, which is very badly planned. Parents die young and here are these little ones left alone; how they will suffer! We feel always insecure. Every second we are dying. Everything passes, the palaces of Caesar and the books of the poets. Animals are scarcely happier than we, and as the dog said when he was put on a chain, " Things are reasonably ordered neither for dogs nor for men."

If only one knew why, it would be a consolation, but the book of life is hard to read. The wise man may succeed in deciphering several chapters, but not the last that treats of the departure into the unknown. We would have to have the philosopher's stone to make the lines shine with a brighter light. Can we find such a stone? They tell us that all evil comes from the error of our first parents, but why should they have made any such mistake?

To all these doubts which work on your mind when you are taking a walk alone, or when you cannot sleep, is added the foolishness of man himself; for the number of fools is too great. Each one believes himself above his condition and swells with pride. The good old snow man, when evening comes, imagines, as we have said, that it is his imperious glance which has forced the sun to sink below the earth. The thistle claims descent from an illustrious Scottish family. The Portuguese duck believes herself of a superior species and despises those that are not Portuguese. The nettle proclaims that it is a distinguished plant since a delicate muslin is woven from it. And so forth, step by step, up to and including the fools who admire the Emperor's invisible clothes.

An excess of work not only makes hands callous, it may embitter the soul. Those who have no work to do risk becoming selfish and cruel. There are maidens, like the little Inger, who walk on bread to avoid soiling their slippers. "The Marsh King's Daughter" points out this double nature that is in us.

Some magic power had a terrible hold over the little one. In the daytime she was as beautiful as any fairy, but had a bad, wicked temper. At night, on the other hand, she became a hideous toad, quiet and pathetic, with sad, mournful eyes. There were two natures in her both in soul and body continually shifting.

In short, all that would not be a very pleasant sight if we saw nothing else in it. In the words of the gingerbread merchant:

I had two young gingerbread people in the window of my shop; one a man with a hat, the other a young lady without a hat. They had a human face only on one side and were not to be looked at from the other. What is more, men are like that and it is not kind to look at their wrong side.

That is what the storyteller in love with nature is thinking about, the animater of things who has himself known pain. Andersen is not one of those saints who, shivering, insist that it is always warm on this earth. He knows the meaning of life. He states resolutely the problem of evil, the problem of existence. But far from being discouraged by the truth, he seeks to release it, to face it. Truth distresses us only when we have a half knowledge of it.

Pondering over existence, he understands that we are in a transitory state from which we cannot escape except through will, faith, love. The human world is only a process of evolution, a chance for us to meet the supreme realities that await us, or at least to prepare ourselves for them. Love, true love, is stronger than absence, stronger than sorrow; it accomplishes all miracles, even that of resurrection. It is the divine spark, symbol of eternal life. Through love, spells are broken. As foretold by the oracle, the King of Egypt, through the power of his daughter's love, came back to life. " Love produces life; from the most ardent love is born the noblest life. It is love only that can save the king's life." Through love, through total sacrifice, having almost given up hope, the little mermaid won immortality. The real evil is the sin against the spirit, the lack of kindness, of humanity. The real good is the aspiration to a higher state to which men of good will shall be admitted and the animals, yes, the animals themselves. " The animal is, like man, a creature of God, and, I believe firmly, no life will be lost, each creature will receive the happiness that it is capable of receiving."

Once there was a hideous toad with a splendid diamond set in its head; always he aspired towards the best.

This precious stone, seek it in the sun, look at it if you can. You will not be able to, the light of the heavenly body is too bright. We have not yet the light that we need to recognize ourselves in the midst of the marvels that God has created. But we shall possess it some day. And then it will be the most beautiful of all the tales; it will be true.

It is this inner life that gives the *Tales* their deep quality. From it also comes that exaltation which spreads through the soul of the readers. From it comes, finally, a marked quality of serenity. I know only one other author who, all differences taken into consideration, creates a similar impression. Manzoni, like Andersen, admitting only as a human weakness the confusion into which the fact of evil throws him, overcomes this state of doubt, and through faith arrives at serenity. Both, before the world spectacle, possess peace. They even allow themselves humor, gaiety, because they hold the secret: " Have faith and hope; they will not deceive you." Both turn by choice towards the humble, because the hierarchy established in this transient world is only an illusion destined to be replaced by a higher law of justice. " The love of the Creator is infinite and embraces equally everything that lives and moves in Him." "All creatures are equal before the infinite love of the Almighty and the same justice governs all the universe." One feels the same Biblical inspiration moving through both Andersen and Manzoni.

The teller of tales stands at his window. He listens to the swallows and the storks that have returned to

Denmark for the fine summer days. He listens to his friend the wind. Or, he mingles with the crowd and listens once more to what the gingerbread merchant is relating, to what the old eel fisherman is telling. He makes use of everything. He tells them again in his own way, these stories that provoke a smile or a tear. He gives them a lyrical style, dramatic and always simple, a style of which he alone is master. He adorns them with brighter and more delicate colors; and, lending them wings, he sends them to the very limits of the world. But he fills them also with intense feeling and therein, without doubt, added to all the other qualities, lies the final attainment which explains their great power.

The children are not mistaken. In these beautiful tales they find not only pleasure, but the law of their being and the feeling of the great role they have to fill. They themselves have been subjected to sorrow. They sense evil confusedly around them, in them; but this vivid suffering is only transitory and not enough to trouble their serenity. Their mission is to bring to the world a renewal of faith and hope. What would become of the human spirit if it were not refreshed by this confident young strength? The new generation arrives to make the world beautiful once more. Everything grows green again. Life finds its reasons for enduring. Andersen, imbuing his tales with an invincible belief in a better future, communes with the soul of children, harmonizes himself with their deep nature, allies himself with their mission. He upholds, with them and through them, the ideal forces which save humanity from perishing.

Childhood North and South

How can we explain this considerate care, these sacrifices, this loving eagerness; this abundance of great authors who have written for childhood — to speak only of the very great: Oliver Goldsmith, Charles and Mary Lamb, Walter Scott, Robert Louis Stevenson, Dickens, Ruskin, Kipling; Washington Irving, Hawthorne, Mark Twain; Pushkin, Gogol, Chekhov; in a word, this superiority of the North over the South?

Is there more tenderness under misty skies? Is affection felt more spontaneously for the weak, the humble, the simple? Are children a rarer product at Tornio than at Naples? Whichever hypothesis we prefer, we must take account of a certain difference in perspective which may be about as follows.

In the Latin countries, children are only small candidates for the career of man. Just as we see passing through the streets of Rome ten-year-old seminarists, wearing the cassock and the beaver hat, just so each of our children is rigged out with his future. The present does not count; the first years are absorbed by those that will follow; they have no value in themselves, they are useful only as preparation. As far back as I can remember, I was always preparing for something: compositions, examinations; even the first communion took on an aspect of competition, with places and ranks. The ideal of Latin education is to watch over the child, never to give him freedom. That file of prisoners, taking those supervised walks on the highways Sundays and Thursdays, what a nightmare! Even in family life, the tenderest maternal advice is translated into orders and prohibitions. Do not walk on the lawn, do not go away, do not soil your hands, do not spot your white frock. It is not that we do not spoil the children. With an air of authority, we gladly indulge their whims. But there is one whim we do not tolerate, that of letting them be themselves.

Among Anglo-Saxons, childhood has the right to exist, and this gives them all through life the nostalgia of a lost paradise. Why hasten to leave such a happy state? With their way of settling down comfortably wherever they find themselves, they settle down into childhood. It possesses a value in itself, a lasting value. The arrival means less than the journey, the journey to springtime. Joy of the body that develops in the open air on green lawns. Peaceful joy of a spirit that knows nothing of overloading or weariness. Joy of a will that obeys only itself, its code of comradeship, its code of honor. Deep joy of a creature lulled by the sweetness of the passing days and who, at the age when time does not yet hurry towards an end we anxiously sense, has not yet learned how the future attacks and lays waste the present.

No being is happier than a young English boy at Eton or Rugby, in short black jacket, or an undergraduate in slacks, strolling on the campus of some American university, Yale, Princeton or Harvard. Even outside these happy isles, the children look out for themselves. They detach themselves from their elders, without feeling obliged to follow in their wake, as in Europe. Let these people (the ones who are growing old and upon whom they look down a little) have their friends, their contacts, that is well and good; but it is fair also that we have ours, they think. Let each go his own way. It is a matter of two different groups whom the years separate. They are on good terms with each other, but each is busy with his own affairs, his own pleasures.

Our son will be going to Paris next summer.

You will send him to us, won't you?

Surely.

We will receive him, we will entertain him. He is a delightful boy, and his parents are real friends of ours. They have been so kind to us in America that we shall be happy to show them our gratitude in Paris.

We wait for him in vain. He came, we know that, but he does not ring our doorbell. In Paris he goes to see friends of his own age, he lives with them. His parents' friends, that is different. He will go back to Chicago without even dreaming of coming to see us.

If either group encroaches upon the other and so marks its superiority, it is not the grownups. This time the scene takes place in Boston. Again it is a matter of very dear friends, with whom we were so intimate that we used to go to see them at whatever hour of the day we chose. We arrive and, strangely enough, they invite us to come up to the second floor. The parents have taken refuge in their bedroom, they have even had their dinner brought up there. The children are entertaining, so the dining room and drawing room belong to them. Discreet parents, well brought up parents, do not embarrass by their presence, will not even show themselves. They understand perfectly that the two kingdoms, the young and the old, must remain separate.

If among the peoples of the North the literature for childhood is superior to that of the peoples of the South, this superiority emanates from an imagination of a different quality. Among the former it is more intimate and more subtle, just as their less brilliant landscapes are those that painters prefer, because they offer a more delicate range of colors. Imagination closer to dreaming, less materialistic, less coördinated, less logical, less detached from the emotional life to which it always reverts, and as a whole, more qualified to attract young souls. The Latins possess a more external imagination, one more accustomed to expressing itself in material and plastic forms, more obedient to reason, even in its caprices, even in its grotesques which are still geometric forms; more dazzling, less poetic, contented less easily, in the sense that it does not find complete satisfaction in its own amusements, but is eager to translate through beauty that promise of happiness that children know nothing about and which is called voluptuousness.

But the superiority of the North is due, above all, to the fact that the Latins lack a certain feeling for childhood, for childhood understood as a fortunate island where happiness must be protected, like an independent republic living according to its own laws, like a caste with glorious privileges. The Latins begin to relax, to breathe, really to live only when they have reached man's estate. Before that they are merely growing, a process that the Latin children themselves finish gladly. If you look at the physiognomy, ages being the same, of a young Spaniard, of a young Italian, of a young French boy, on the one hand and on the other hand, at the physiognomy of a young English boy, of a young American, you will notice how the former is already more mature. In the same way, the mind of the former is farther advanced, as they say; farther advanced on the road of life.

In countries where stalks grow more slowly because the sunlight is weaker, in countries where adults wear out more quickly from the time they begin life's struggle, they encourage childhood to last longer. They judge the early age happy, not because it does not know reality, but because it experiences a reality better adapted to the consciousness that it has of itself. The ideal of life is not an inaccessible future, but simple happiness, immediate, tangible. Youth possesses it; it would be a crime to take it away. For the Latins, children have never been anything but future men. The Nordics have understood better this truer truth, that men are only grown-up children.

IV

NATIONAL TRAITS

The Italy of Yesterday

W E can disregard the literature for childhood only if we consider unimportant the way in which a national soul is formed and sustained.

In that first book in Italy to be written wholly from a child's point of view, the illustrious Pinocchio is a marionette, slim, lively, prancing about, dressed in a jacket of flowered paper, with shoes made of bark and a hat made of bread. Once upon a time a carpenter wanted to make a table leg out of a piece of wood. But at the very moment he was cutting it, he heard a small voice that said: " Stop, you are hurting me! " As he was planing the wood, the same voice spoke again, " Stop, you are tickling me! "

The carpenter, afraid of this talkative piece of wood, handed it over gladly to his crony Geppetto, who was planning just then to make a marionette. Geppetto carried the gift to his humble home and set about the task of making a masterpiece. " I will call him," said he, "Pinocchio. This name will make his fortune. I knew a whole family of Pinocchi: Pinocchio the father, Pinocchia the mother, Pinocchi the children; they all lived very comfortably; the richest of them begged for alms."

Then he carved a head, hair, forehead, eyes. Hardly had he finished the nose, than it lengthened out of all proportion. In vain he cut it again. The nose always stayed too long and too pointed. Hardly had he finished the mouth than it began to laugh; the hands, than they stole his wig; the feet, than Pinocchio made for the door and escaped; showing in this way his longing to see the world, and his impatience to make friends with the little Italians.

Young souls, still tender and unformed, in whom virtue is as yet only an instinct, in whom vices are as yet only faults, need help in asserting themselves. They are enraptured when they see and recognize themselves in a book. They see themselves as though in a mirror. Pinocchio is not bad; and if it were enough to have good intentions to be perfect, Pinocchio would be a paragon. But he is weak. He declares openly that we ought not to resist temptation because it is a waste of time. What he is forbidden to do is always a little more attractive than what he is ordered to do. Repentance follows close on sinning, but sinning follows close on repentance. He would prefer to have knowledge without the effort of learning. For some time he lives in a carefree country whose charms are lauded by a friend. They have no school there on Thursday or Sunday, and the weeks are made up of one Sunday and six Thursdays. The long vacations last from the first of January to the thirty-first of December. They have a good time all day long. At evening they go to bed and the next day they begin all over again.

Pinocchio does not object to telling white lies to conceal his peccadillos. He confesses the truth only when his nose, his long, pointed nose, lengthens out immoderately. Pinocchio is a boaster. He claims he can handle the assassins all by himself, but almost before he sees their shadow, he takes to his heels desperately. Like his little friends, Pinocchio is pugnacious and ready to claim his rights by the strength of his fists. Like them, Pinocchio loves practical jokes, except those they play on him. He is full of self-esteem, likes to be in the limelight, but is not unwilling to admit he is wrong when caught in escapades.

All the fixations which a child has, such as not taking medicine or not wanting to eat lentils, although he has never tasted them; all the little selfishnesses that cunningly grow strong roots if they are not pulled up before it is too late; all the good qualities of childhood also, the sincere and deep affection, a confiding heart as yet undeceived, the need of being loved which calls forth love: all that is so clear that even a ten-year-old reader could not fail to understand Pinocchio the clever, the subtle and the loving.

Here is a magic mirror creating an illusion by playing around the truth. How boring the world is as grownups represent it! Obstacles to dreams everywhere, sometimes truth, sometimes probability. And categories everywhere: on the highest plane, man who has crowned himself king; on a lower plane, animals, plants, and everything included in that vague substance called matter. Children, on the contrary, never discolor, limit or classify the universe. They attribute to it the same superabundance of life that is in themselves so that everything moves before their eyes, everything speaks to their attentive ears, nothing restrains their fancy.

Pinocchio joyfully leads them on through the unexpected and the extraordinary. He leads them to the marionette theatre where his brothers, the puppets, recognize him so readily that they give him a hearty welcome, light up the candles again after the show and dance with him until daybreak. He directs them towards the town of Fool-Catchers where they meet only ragged dogs, shabby butterflies who have sold the gold powder on their wings; cocks without combs and peacocks without feathers. They see the Beggars' Field where the Cat and the Fox, hypocrites that they are, claim that five crown pieces buried at the foot of a tree will produce a harvest of gold, if only they are watered carefully. Whatever happens, the story always rebounds, light and whimsical. It seems to stop, it starts off again. As Pinocchio himself would say, there are only beginnings, never endings, except on the last page.

The story tells how Pinocchio has his leg caught in a snare, stealing grapes, and how, set free by the owner, he has to take the place of the watchdog with a big collar around his neck. It tells how he was changed into an ass, appeared in a circus as a performing animal and risked having his skin made into a drum. It tells how the Fisherman, taking him for a fish of an unknown species, had him coated with flour and was all ready to throw him on the stove. It tells how he was swallowed by the *pescecane*, the dogfish, the shark that devours those who are not good. And it tells many other adventures that include the Mastiff, the Crow and the Owl, the Black Rabbits, the courteous Dolphin and the Snail who takes seven hours to crawl from the third to the ground floor. Stretched out in a fairy coach drawn by a hundred white mice, carried through the air on a dove's back, shamefully dragged along by two policemen, in perpetual motion, Pinocchio travels the realms of imagination.

Is not imagination, in fact, one of the most pleasing characteristics of the Italian spirit? What people have used their fancy to build more fairylike structures? Serious while describing the circles of Hell, laughing while sowing flowers in the gardens of Armida, brilliant and as though rejoicing over its own apotheosis in the melodramas of Metastasio, the Italian imagination is a magnificent heritage of which Pinocchio has received his share and spent it profitably. His physical equipment which might bind him to the earth is reduced to a minimum; hard wood and springs; no weighty body to hold back his caprices. He is as light and lively as spirit. He is as little obedient to the laws of dull existence as an association of ideas is to those of logic. He has the mobility of the creatures that stir in our dreams, being himself a dream in the night of a child.

Before he was called Pinocchio and amused youngsters, he was Harlequin, Punchinello, or Stenterello. He was one of the *maschere,* changeless characters that served as a fixed point for improvisation. That sparkling Italian comedy, enjoyed and borrowed by the French for years because they could not imitate it, lives again in this nimble marionette. It reminds us of those comedies in which the ingenuity of the players, fragmentary action, hot-headed impulse, and *brio* are given a free field.

We still attribute to the Italy of yesterday, so recent but already so remote, an opportunism which was a part of its character, a custom, a dogma of its politics. Not heroism, but realistic and immediate self-interest. Mock who will the petty traders, they are the ones who win out in the end. Would our Pinocchio by chance be an opportunist?

Let us admit that his morality is neither sublime nor even superior. It is practical. If we were to sum up the philosophy of the book, we should get something like this: There is an imminent justice that rewards good and punishes evil. Since good is advantageous we must prefer it. The child who fights with his comrades or who plays hooky, or who listens to the advice of chance friends rather than obey his parents, or who does not keep his promises, will be punished for his misdeeds. The chastisements will come in unexpected ways but without fail. The child who thinks only of drinking, eating, and being a vagabond all day long, ends in prison or in the hospital. Money does not fall from heaven. It must be earned painfully by work with the hands or mind. Only imbeciles can believe that it is acquired by easy processes. They are the dupes of rascals.

Social morality is reduced to a law of exchange. To show oneself to be nice, kind, generous, is to assure oneself of being repaid in kind. " The other person " is the innumerable and mysterious being who appears grateful when he has been well treated, but who forgets neither wrongs nor injuries. Two proverbs keep recurring in the story: *quel ch'è fatto, è reso:* Tit for tat; *i casi son tanti:* No knowing what may happen.

This whimsical imagination, and this very practical sense of a way of life, are not necessarily incompatible. And we can very well conceive a psychology subtle enough to pass rapidly from the realm of dreams to that of concrete realities. These lively minds, who enjoy giving color to commonplace beings and things, are never deluded by the illusion that they create for themselves. They destroy it as easily as they create it, as is the case here. Can we be sure that this simple and practical way of understanding morality is not an attribute of the whole Italian nation? Could it be a special form of that " profound good sense " so often presented as one of the most fundamental traits of the race?

But Pinocchio is not only Italian; he is Tuscan, like his father Collodi — Collodi's real name being Carlo Lorenzini. The author published the amusing story in the *Giornale dei Bambini* in 1880. I challenge you to find a Tuscan who is not witty and spirited. All of them, even the common people, even the peasants, even the youngsters, have a flair for detecting the ridiculous, seizing any chance to launch a witticism. Witticisms, absurd associations of ideas, humorous observations, are to be found on every page in Pinocchio; an exuberant imagination that is not only comical but keen; a mixture of apparent naïveté and caustic shrewdness, such as we French have in our Guignol; but ours is not so light, for the Tuscan wit is subtle and shrewd in a different way. Here is one of their simple jokes: —

" What is your father's name? "

" Geppetto."

" What trade does he ply? "

" That of being poor."

And we have also this criticism, merely suggested, of a petty and very human fault when the fairy with blue hair invites Pinocchio's friends to tea: " Some of them had to be urged, but when they knew that the rolls were to be buttered even on the outside, they all ended by saying: 'We will come, too, to give you pleasure.'" How many people give pleasure to others in order to give themselves pleasure! There are funnier lines, like the story of the marionette showman, a man terrible in appearance but good-hearted, who cannot keep from sneezing when he is secretly moved. There are some that are more stressed. Pinocchio has been put in prison because he is innocent. It happens, on a special occasion, that all the guilty are given their liberty. Pinocchio wants to leave, too.

" Not you," says the jailer; " you are not one of them."

" I beg your pardon," replies Pinocchio; " I, too, am a rascal."

" Then it is perfectly all right," says the jailer.

And respectfully doffing his cap he bowed, opened the doors and let Pinocchio depart.

" I have another hunger," cries Pinocchio, one day when he was insufficiently filled. In the same way, Collodi always holds in reserve another kind of laughter and wit. In the gardens of some Tuscan town, against a background of rising hills, some morning in spring under a pale sky, a statue should be erected to Collodi. It would show the artist in the act of carving his famous puppet out of wood. . . . What am I saying? Another statue? Heaven forbid, there are too many already and they are too ugly. We should instead celebrate very simply every April Pinocchio's anniversary. There would be no speech. There would be dances and songs; there would be a marionette show, games of every kind, and lots of candy, cakes and sweet drinks; and liberty and gaiety and even joy. Beautiful picture, appropriate for the Italy of yesterday.

The Italy of today is vehement and bellicose. She is oratorical and always has been; but her eloquence has taken on a vibrant and moving quality that keeps the people in a state of exaltation. She has made a doctrine of force. She takes pleasure in announcing openly her next conquests. And that, for those who do not know her well, is a great change.

But those who understand her a little know that her present psychology can be explained by a sentiment that has been growing for centuries, following a logical curve now reaching its vertex. Italy has been disunited for too long a time, subject to foreign powers and, what hurts more than anything, despised. She has been " treated as a slave." The Risorgimento was her revenge but an incomplete one. Even the First World War did not appease her. She is dissatisfied with herself. So she wants to assert herself still more; to become by force one of the dominating powers of Europe and of the world, and to plan an imperial role. Then, and then only, will Italian pride be satisfied.

In January, 1886, De Amicis, who was already a favorite with the public — author among other works of army tales that had made a fortune — went to call for his son as school was letting out. De Amicis saw him coming with a classmate, a little poor boy weirdly clothed in garments much too big. Before parting the two children kissed each other. De Amicis, moved by this friendly act, conceived at once an idea for a book depicting school life. In four months the manuscript was finished, and handed over to the printer. *Cuore* was born and Italian youth had a book that interpreted its fondest aspirations.

Life at school, besides being glowingly depicted with many amusing scenes, is thoroughly imbued with *Italianità* and above everything else this book for children is a breviary of patriotism. On the one hand it settles the balance sheet of the past. The fact dominating Italian history being the fulfilment of unity, it is important that the feeling of this unity pass into the child consciousness. The setting is in Turin and more than one detail brings Piedmontese customs to mind. In the very first week of the school year, the head master comes into the class to present a young Calabrian, a newcomer.

The master speaks: " Do not forget what I am telling you. In order that a Calabrian child may feel at home in Turin, and that a child from Turin may feel at home in Reggio Calabria, our country has struggled for fifty years and thirty thousand Italians have died. . . . " Hardly had the Calabrian sat down in his place before his neighbors gave him some pen-points and a picture and a pupil on the rear bench had passed a Swedish stamp along to him.

In the same way, on the day for distributing prizes, the pupils assigned the envied mission of carrying the volumes to the authorities, who in turn hand them to the laureates, are not chosen haphazardly. They select a Milanese, a Florentine, a Roman, a Neapolitan, a Sicilian, a Sardinian; a representation of Italian unity. The entire fatherland, through this symbol, will attend the festivity. Every month the master reads a tale, to the great joy of the school group. Let us look at the titles: *The Little Patriot of Padua; The Little Sentry from Lombardy; The Little Copyist*

from Florence; The Little Drummer from Sardinia.
Any child who has made *Cuore* his favorite book will
feel no sentiment more deeply than patriotism.

But of what use would this balance sheet be, on the
other hand, if it did not bear on the future? The essence of patriotism, as De Amicis conceives it, is not
peaceful and quiet; it is still a wounded feeling in spite
of the affirmation of victory. It never expresses itself
except in a tone of singular exaltation. Fathers of
families, mothers and children themselves make a
lyrical or epic theme of it. The contents, far from
being exhausted, are just beginning to spread abroad.

It is not the peaceful assurance, for example, that
one would find in an Englishman. The Italian must
show off, stir about, exert himself. That is the kind
of intensity, of emotivity, that he calls action. It is
a dynamic force. From the moment it is acquired,
this unity forms a new point of departure. It shall
stimulate progress towards a higher destiny. One
day's march is done, another is making ready, the very
one that the Italy of today is striving to attain.

France

Who has not spoken of our passion for logic?

Let us consider the fairies as Charles Perrault has
depicted them. They could, if they wished, frolic to
their heart's content, indulge in all the roguish delights of the unexpected and the contradictory instead of allowing even the miraculous to be governed
by cold reason. Who would hinder them if they
chose to make caprice the sole ruler of their winged
existence? Nobody, certainly. But they are French
fairies, so it pleases them to pursue in the concrete,

which is their sphere of action, the law of logical adaptation and abstract harmony. "Someone has even ingeniously remarked," writes Fernand Baldensperger in his book on the psychology of *La Littérature,* "that the fairies of Perrault are, in their way, Cartesian fairies. Their charming wand can perform the most extravagant metamorphoses. The Asiatic fancy, indeed, does not refuse to bring forth an enchanted palace from a pebble, or a princess from a swan's feather fluttering about in the cold wind. But our fairies work at a similar theme as if fancy were being governed by common sense. And so it has to be a well-rounded and well-ripened pumpkin which is transformed for Cinderella's ball into a beautiful golden coach, and a large-whiskered rat that is changed into a moustached coachman. We see here the timidity and logic of rational fairies who take care not to confuse appearances and analogies for the empty pleasure of displaying their authority and who are willing to sacrifice some of their power for the subtle pleasure of showing respect for the logical concepts of things."

The observation is absolutely correct. Re-read the passage in which Perrault shows us poor Cinderella in tears, because her sisters have departed for the ball, while she, a despised kitchen-maid, remains at home a prisoner:

"Well now! If you will be a good girl," said her godmother, "I will see that you get there." She led her into her room and said to her: "Go out to the garden and bring me back a pumpkin." Cinderella went at once to gather the handsomest one she could find and brought it to her godmother, unable to imagine how this pumpkin could enable her to go to the ball. Her godmother hollowed it out and having left nothing but the shell, struck it with her wand and the pumpkin was changed immediately into a beautiful golden coach. Then she went to look in the mousetrap where she found six live mice; she told Cinderella to open cautiously the door of the mousetrap, and as each mouse came out, she touched it with her wand and the mouse was immediately changed into a fine horse; that made a beautiful coach and six horses of a handsome, dappled mouse gray.

The golden pumpkin becomes a golden coach, the mice become mouse-gray horses, the moustached rat becomes a coachman embellished with a magnificent moustache, the lizards become lackeys bedizened with braid. Cinderella's godmother has sequence in her ideas; she observes the proper rules, and the French are satisfied. For they are less fond of being dazzled than of seeing clearly.

They say that, next to logic, what characterizes us most is our wit. If there are nations lacking in that quality, ours has enough to spare. Some even find we have too much. The Frenchman owes it to himself, by definition, to be witty the moment he comes into the world.

As in the story of " Riquet of the Tuft ":

Once upon a time there was a Queen who bore a son so ugly and ill-formed that people doubted for a long time if he was a human being at all. A fairy who was there when he was born promised that he would be charming because he would be witty and clever. She added that by virtue of the fairy gift she had given him he would be able to make the woman he loved as clever as himself. This child could hardly talk before he said countless pretty things with a wit that charmed everyone.

123

Our Riquet becomes as affected as Marivaux. Listen to him paying court to the Princess who is as stupid as she is beautiful:

"Beauty," went on Riquet of the Tuft, "is so great a gift that surely it should take the place of everything else: and when one possesses it, I know nothing that would be worth worrying about."

"I would rather," said the Princess, "be as ugly as you are, and be witty, than possess the beauty that I do and be as stupid as I am."

"There is nothing, Madame, which shows more clearly that one has wit than to believe one does not have it; and it is in the nature of this virtue that, the more one has of it, the more one believes oneself lacking it."

Then there is our special way of organizing a story. Hop o' My Thumb does not prove himself as fore-sighted as he thinks when he scatters bread crumbs along his path and the birds fly down and eat them up. But though his hardship may be extreme, and his situation desperate, do not worry: he will fall on his feet.

There is the important place that woman holds in the history of our civilization. And in all our tales there are so many gallant heroes, so many kings' sons who know to perfection how to win their ladies with madrigals. So many princesses—Finette, Gracieuse, La Belle aux cheveux d'or, Florine, Désirée, and all the rest. It is not enough for them to be pretty; they must be subtle and wise as well; and the most beautiful maiden in the world cannot please us if she lacks the gift of repartee. Above all they must not be arrogant and proud; that is the fault which we as a people do not forgive. One could compose, from our fairy tales alone, an amusing portrait of French women as Frenchmen like them. Coming down from the dim past, they have passed through Versailles, through Paris, before reaching us; and we have interpreted them in our own fashion.

We have a certain ingenuity that spurs us on to small discoveries and sometimes to big ones. There was Jules Verne, who went around the world in eighty days, traveled twenty thousand leagues under the sea, and remained in a balloon for five weeks, all without leaving Amiens. Only by a hair's breadth he missed discovering that by taking advantage of the differences in temperature at various depths of oceans, cold could be manufactured and, in doing so, the condition of continents changed and our globe transformed. At least he went to the very center of the earth to see what was going on there.

There is our sociability. And the Countess de Ségur. In her books you will not find the description of an individual, preoccupied with his ego, but that of a given society. Her skill consisted in gathering her characters into a social group, improving them, polishing them, fashioning them into an agreeable and useful ensemble. Her widows and widowers remarry. She leads General Dourakine, alone in life, to the Inn of the Guardian Angel.[1]

I am aware that her maiden name was Rostopchine and that traits peculiar to her own Russia have often been brought out in her stories. Her conception of authority is very different from ours. Any order coming from above is sacred; it must be executed at once, or beware blows or even the knout. General Dourakine is very evidently not one of us. This worthy gentleman belongs to our race neither through his virtues

[1] *A l'Auberge de l'Ange Gardien* by Comtesse de Ségur.

nor his faults; the like are never seen beneath the prudent, peaceful and clear sky of *l'Ile de France*. He needs a long acclimatization to soothe his outbursts, appease his fits of rage and adapt his Russian soul to French ways.

The characters the good Countess sets on the stage would easily lack restraint if she did not watch out. Sometimes she does forget to watch out. What an appetite! What a stomach! Listen to this simple picnic luncheon: " First they cut into an enormous hare pie, then jellied meats, then potatoes with salt, some ham, some crayfish, plum tart and finally cheese and fruits." That is the way food is provided in countries with a harsh climate, where the plant called man has to be vigorously re-victualed. We French are not in the habit of carrying about as much as all that when we want to eat on the grass.

Neither is it in us to mix a dash of cruelty with pleasure. We are not so complicated or so morbid. Two children are joyfully reviewing their vacation as follows:

Marguerite:

And that poor toad that we buried in an ant hill!

Rudy:

And that little bird that I took out of its nest for you and that died because I squeezed it too tightly!

Characteristics of this sort can be found in Madame de Ségur without much difficulty and they do not belong to us; they reflect another country. But she was French also and, as such, loved society, drawing rooms, castles, fine parks to stroll in while conversing. How pleasant it was to talk, passing lightly from one subject to another with easy grace, accepting your companion's point of view as foil to your own, welcoming another personality as an extension of one's own personality and accomplishing this with elegance, gaiety and wit. No pastime is more delightful, as Madame de Ségur knows well. Her personages are members of Society. We can visualize them in the salons of the Restoration or of the Second Empire; the men are gathered about the hearth, the women seated in easy chairs, all of them playing at conversation. It is a curious fact, and difficult to explain at first, that Madame de Ségur has remained in favor, not only with our rich children, but with the poor as well. Even foreigners, Orientals, who live in the sordid sections of Paris, read with delight *Les Petites Filles Modèles* or *Les Vacances*.

How does that happen? Because poor children find in these books the revelation of a world that they had never imagined by themselves, so greatly does it differ from the one that surrounds them; of an astonishing, dazzling world with great ladies, titled gentlemen, little girls with fine manners and beautiful speech; gaily lighted salons, fetes on the lawn, visits, promenades, dinners, luncheons; parasols and crinolines, redingotes and side-whiskers; a complete picture of the aristocracy that continues to delight children today, because it seems to them hardly less strange and beautiful than the world inhabited by the Prince Charmings and the Princesses in the fairy tales. I own a very curious testimonial; it is a paper written by a nine-year-old girl with an obviously Jewish name who was asked at school to name her favorite books:

I like very much the story of *Sans Famille*, by Hector Malot, which I have read with great interest from beginning to end.

At the beginning it made me very sad, but at the end I was very happy for Remi finds his mother again.

Also I like very much the books in the *Bibliothèque Rose*, those by the Countess de Ségur, especially *Les Vacances*, *Les Malheurs de Sophie*, *Un Bon Petit Diable*, *Les Petites Filles Modèles* and many others.

Of all these books I like best *Les Petites Filles Modèles* because the author shows how they used to live in other days.

The author shows how they used to live! There, it seems, is one of the secrets of its persistent charm.

We could go on in this vein indefinitely if we were not in a hurry to reach the fortunate isle of books for young people. England, more than any other country, has implanted its own eternal characteristics within the covers of its children's books.

England

England could be reconstructed entirely from its children's books. We learn at once from them that John Bull was never ashamed to say his prayers, to go to church or to brood in his conscience over religious problems. Turning over the pages of the books that he gave his sons and daughters in the course of the nineteenth century would be enough to convince us. And if we wanted further proof we could look back through the years and see what a flowering of books, even more affectedly pious than devout, were produced towards the end of the seventeenth century and the beginning of the eighteenth. What do I mean by that? In an epoch when there was as yet nothing written just for children, there was, nevertheless, in England, a book that presented the problem of salvation to them in a tragic and haunting manner. I am not speaking of the Bible, which was, and remains, the first of all their readings, but of an imaginative work that was not written for them, and of which they took possession according to their custom: the work of a creative mystic, setting forth in allegory, almost in the form of a novel, the life story of the Christian pilgrim.

The book was born out of a country's crisis and a soul's crisis. Published in 1678, it had been written several years before in prison by John Bunyan, who was being punished for his faith. He was the son of a poor tinsmith, and he became a tinsmith, and later a soldier, until the day when he examined his conscience, judged himself the most abominable of unbelievers, found in the Gospel reasons for hoping and living and decided to consecrate himself to the redemption of sinners. He went about preaching, baptizing, was persecuted, imprisoned, but always returned to his vocation as a shepherd of souls as soon as he was free, and gave to the immense crowd of dissenters that *Pilgrim's Progress* which caused him to be venerated as one of God's prophets.

Unhappy pilgrim, born with the dangerous privilege of being a believer! His ideas and emotions take on such irresistible color and shape that he pictures the terrors of doubt and the aspirations of faith with vivid realism. He discovers a symbol of eternal life in every event of our mortal existence. He tells us how he lived, like all his brothers, in the City of Destruction, without even realizing his wretched state. But one day he felt the burden of his sins lying heavy on his shoulders, a burden so heavy that it bowed him down to the ground, that it risked making him fall lower than the sepulchre, into the infernal abyss. Then he uttered a cry of despair: What can I do to deserve salvation?

He must go away, travel, crushed as he is by his burden. Leave his wife, his children, his friends, his fellow citizens, all those who want to bind him with earthly chains. He must go away and begin humbly the pilgrimage which will lead him towards the celestial light that the Evangelist points out to him in the distance, in the direction of Holy Zion.

So a long journey begins, filled with agonies, errors, new beginnings, despair and renewed transports. In the Valley of Humiliation, he will battle with the monster Apollyon who is covered with scales, has the wings of a dragon, the paws of a bear; from his belly smoke and flames come forth, his mouth is like the jaw of a lion. In the Castle of Doubt the Giant Despair will throw him into a dungeon, where he will remain for long days without bread and without water. Victor over obstacles constantly reappearing, again and again he risks losing his way: Worldly Wisdom, Hypocrisy, Flattery lead him astray. His weakness is infinite, but his Faith rouses the intervention of good Angels who prevail against the plots of the Devil, and Christian finally passes through the gates of the City of Light; at great risk since, even in sight of the goal, he tells us, one can lose everything gained by the journey and slip down into the very depths of Hell.

It is a book of faith, certainly, but it is also a book of fear, depicting with an indefinable, sombre joy the evil powers capable of changing the pious pilgrimage into one of damnation. It is a book which, as it goes along, dwells on human misery as if to relish it before pointing out a way to heal it. It is a reassuring allegory, but disturbing also, in that it makes the attainment of salvation seem like miraculous luck. It is a spiritual flame that a gust of storm threatens and beats down and that again mounts upwards to flicker anew. It is the contest of a troubled conscience, for which the religious problem is not only the most important but the only one in life.

The pilgrim left his wife and four children at home. As if he had not had enough on the first journey, and as if eager to renew the emotions, the fears, the terrors he enjoyed in the first book, John Bunyan begins his tale again. Christiana takes to the road in her turn; a road where the shadow of equally formidable monsters is projected, but which is made easy by the intervention of supernatural personages and that at last leads Christiana towards the Celestial City where, clothed in the garment of immortality, she will find God. Why should not children, always attracted by vivid color, have been eager to behold such imagery, so naïve and powerful in its sincerity, and why should not such imagery sustain the ardent and sombre faith of a Puritan heart?

But once outside the church or the chapel, after having read the Gospel, listened to the sermon, chanted the Psalms, the Englishman again turns to the realities of the world here below and does not reject them. Since he cannot change them, he is at least going to organize them for his own benefit. For him life is not what it was for his neighbors on the other side of the Channel — a theorem for which it is important first of all to find the solution, a logical form that must be forced on rebel matter, a fundamental principle that must be asserted against the claims of men and things. For him it is, far more, a vast field of action.

Let us face facts, says John Bull to his children. Do not forget, readers, say his books, that there is a vast number of questions to which we shall never reply, not only because the answers are difficult, but because they are useless. Things are what they are. Do not multiply the indiscreet *whys*. The *whys* lead to nothing. Take it easy, do not ask too much of them. Ascertain, attempt, experiment for yourself, that is the thing to do. Who would expect to find here the name of the initiator of the experimental method, the name of the great Bacon? Yet that is the name a certain Maria Edgeworth pronounces in tracing back to her pedagogue father the quality of her own writings. "I claim for my father the credit for having been the first to recommend, by his example, what Lord Bacon would call the experimental system in Education." No fear of her forgetting this system in her own works. Open to " Harry and Lucy,"[1] if you are intrepid:

Harry:

We can try, papa.

The Father:

Yes, my son, it is the only system of learning that is safe. . . .

There was no foolishness in the newspapers published for the English youngsters during the nineteenth century, newspapers that increased in numbers, to the point where they resembled those mythical armies in which each dead soldier was represented by two other living ones. No foolishness but facts; still more facts, serious learning, practical learning. Good biographies. History, especially the history of Eng-

[1] In *Easy Lessons.*

land. Geography, especially the geography of England and its colonies. How things are made. How the postal system and electric bells work. Let superficial nations provide pleasant tales, stories that the newspaper begins and that the subscribers will finish, to show their ingenuity and wit. A serious nation repudiates such futile games; it wants something solid. For example: " The subject that we offer for our first prize in our new series," says *The Boy's Own Paper,* " is the cultivation and manufacture of cotton." Well and good. " The subjects that we offer for our competition," *The Boy's Early Book* says, " are the following: 1. Complete history of the Penny Postal system. 2. History of the Princes of Wales, heirs of the crown of England. 3. Electricity in its application to telegraphy 4. The trapeze, its usefulness in physical training. 5. On the making of clocks and watches. 6. Origin and history of surnames." Good old newspapers, how wise and practical and utilitarian you were! You did not expect, I hope, profound answers to such questions. But you were inviting your readers, placidly, gravely, to carry on the traditions of their ancestors, and your way of amusing them was to teach them what they ought to know in order to become a good merchant at Liverpool, a good manufacturer at Manchester, and a good Englishman everywhere.

These newspapers are often a business, a financial enterprise, a bank or a store. It is not that other countries lack self-interest, but they have the delicacy, or we might say, the hypocrisy, to mention money as little as possible. They prefer to encourage the illusion that the publishers started the enterprise just for pleasure and that the editors continue it out

of pure zeal. Not so the English newspapers. One of
them is like a group of stockholders who hold meet-
ings from time to time and settle their balance sheet.
Another one checks up on its circulation — more than
a hundred thousand copies a week: another little effort and we will go to a hundred and fifty thousand.
What inventiveness they showed at a time when we
may assume that the art of publicity was less aggressive than today, and children less exacting!

I notice that in 1863 *The Boy's Journal, a Magazine of Literature, Science, Adventure and Amusement,* opens a shopping agency. It will send to its
readers, at cost price (as soon as it has received the
amount in stamps or in money orders), everything
that they would like to get for themselves in London
— toys, scientific apparatus, tools, books, drawing
materials, chemical products, engravings, etc. . . .
It will undertake the shipment, it will point out the
best articles at the best price with the best way of
using same. In 1867 the *Boys of England* offer premi-
ums: ten silver watches, fifty concertinas, fifty pairs
of pretty rabbits, a hundred volumes of the complete
works of Shakespeare, a hundred German flutes, a
hundred boxes of dominoes, a thousand engravings
to frame, a hundred beautiful stickpins. Between
rabbits and flutes the works of Shakespeare are not
very well placed, nor are the works of Walter Scott
in a second distribution: two ponies, thirty silver
watches, fifty cricket bats, fifty fishing rods, thirty
weapons for fencing, two hundred volumes of Walter
Scott's novels prettily bound, a hundred engravings
to frame, three splendid Newfoundland dogs. And
the distributions continue.

Is it in the hope of winning a flute or a Newfoundland dog? The fact is that His Royal Highness, Prince Arthur, will soon honor this generous newspaper with his subscription. The newspaper is at once enormously raised in its own esteem. As things are things, without criticism or explanation, so princes are princes; and social hierarchy is social hierarchy: to obtain the subscription of a Royal Highness is a touching honor and a sure profit. What reader in England did not rejoice at the thought that His Royal Highness was reading the gazette to which he had himself subscribed? That Count Wilhelm Bernstorff, son of His Excellency the Ambassador from Prussia, was reading it likewise? And that it was the favorite of the sons of the nobility and gentry in the United Kingdom as well as in the Colonies?

When a duke marries off his daughter, says Salvador de Madariaga in the study he has made of the English character, all England rejoices.

Alice, tired of sitting on the lawn without doing anything, sees a white rabbit with pink eyes pass by, who pulls his watch out of his waistcoat pocket and cries out: " Oh dear! Oh dear! I shall be too late! " She follows him, drops down into his burrow and begins to slip, to tumble down towards unknown depths, perhaps to the very center of the earth. She finds herself in a long hall that looks out on a delightful garden, into which unfortunately she cannot go; the door is too small to pass through. Strange place! If she drinks from a little bottle on which is written: " Drink me," she grows shorter; she folds in on herself like a telescope. If she takes a bite of cake on which is written: " Eat me," she grows tall, taller, until she no longer sees her feet, to which she sends messages in despair. Forever in this marvelous country, Alice will pass from too short to too tall, without finding her right size. There will even be a moment when, after nibbling one or the other side of a phenomenal toadstool, she becomes so short that her chin bumps into her feet with a jerk; or so tall, that she reaches the top of the trees, where a terrified bird takes her for a serpent coming to rob the eggs from her nest. " I am only a little girl," Alice says reassuringly. This little-girl-telescope, who at times is forty feet tall, and at times has no longer any height at all — what distraught fancy has created her?

We shall see many other things in *Alice in Wonderland*. We shall see the White Rabbit reappear always lamenting: " Oh, the Duchess, the Duchess! Won't she be savage if I've kept her waiting! " We shall see Alice swimming in a lake of her own tears, becoming acquainted with incongruous animals that, like herself, are trying to escape from this expanse of water, and playing absurd games with them. We shall see the Duchess' house served by Frog-Footmen and Fish-Footmen. The cook has put so much pepper in the soup, that everyone sneezes. The cook has a mean disposition; she throws at random spade, pincers, poker, plates, saucepans at the Duchess, and at the child that the latter holds on her knees. The Duchess entrusts the child to Alice who wants to put her in a safe place, but the child turns into a young pig and trots away. " We are all mad," says a cat who figures in the hubbub and who is not the least astonishing character, since he has the faculty of appearing or disappearing in the air at will. Perhaps we are not yet entirely mad; but we run a great risk of becoming so, if the story continues.

Unless we, too, enter resolutely into the spirit of the game; unless we relinquish this imperious logic which is in the Latin mentality, but which is not necessarily in that of our English neighbor; unless we consent to live in a lighthearted dream. But is it so distasteful to us? The laughter that a clown's drollery provokes certainly has its charm. It relaxes, rests us, and claiming our entire attention distracts us from life's problems. Let us take things as they come. Let us not insist that the characters walk straight ahead, without deviating, towards a certain goal. If they fade out, if they leave the tale and do not reappear, let them stay where they are, somewhere in the unknowable. Let us not be difficult, but accept everything in good spirit — plays on words, double meanings, jokes that make our hair stand on end, jests, comical transpositions, burlesque tricks. Are they all mad? Perhaps they are wise men, who, freed from the constraints of banks, offices, or even class rooms, libraries and lecture halls, are liberating our spirits. We grow tipsy on freedom, we feel ourselves becoming young again, like Alice; and we are not ashamed of it since in England we are not in a country where old men hold sway.

So let us revel in nonsense. It is good for us; it offers us an interlude of happiness. Let us attend the justly famous tea party where the March Hare, the Dormouse, the Mad Hatter and Alice appear. The Dormouse dozes, wakes up only to mention treacle, and submit to some subtle joke, such as being dipped in the teapot. The March Hare is astonished that his watch does not run, although it is greased with the very best butter. The Hatter shows himself, if I may say so, to be the most stubborn of the group; he is, indeed, entirely unreasonable. He asks riddles that no one can answer because they have no answer, and he is very pleased with himself. Time has stopped; it is always teatime; and they cannot wash the cups since there is no longer any time, so they contentedly change places and start all over again.

The Queen's croquet match is superior, if possible, to the scene of the teacups. Alice ends by entering the garden she has glimpsed at the start of the story. She finds herself in the kingdom of the pack of cards. The first sight that strikes her eye is that of the three gardeners, the Two, the Five and the Seven of Spades, busily painting a white rosebush red; for they have made a mistake in the color, and if the Queen should notice it, she would have them beheaded; so they must repaint the roses. In the midst of a brilliant retinue, in which the White Rabbit figures, arrive the King and Queen of Hearts; the Queen decrees that they shall play croquet.

Alice thought she had never seen such a curious croquet-ground in all her life: it was all ridges and furrows: the croquet-balls were all live hedgehogs and the mallets live flamingoes, and the soldiers had to double themselves up and stand on their hands and feet, to make the arches.

The players all play at once, bumping into each other and fighting for the hedgehogs that are making off. The flamingo-mallets turn their heads at the moment one prepares to hit. The card soldiers, tired, take their natural positions again and stroll about. Indescribable tumult; every minute, or almost, the voice of the Queen is heard: " Off with his head. . . ." All the players are thus condemned to death and there remain only the King, the Queen and Alice. That, however, is of no importance since when all is said and done the guilty are all pardoned.

Nothing could be more specifically English than the humor. Humor, being always a contradiction between what one says and what one seems to say, is often a serious way of expressing amusing things, but it can also be an amusing way of expressing serious things. I appeal to all those who have ever given themselves up to that infernal pastime called croquet. Every croquet match resembles that of the Queen's, either for the furies that it arouses if one takes it tragically (Off with his head!) or for the indescribable tumult which usually interrupts the game. And so the description that one finds of it in *Alice in Wonderland* has its share of resemblance and truth. Likewise, nobody will claim that the conversations held around a cup of tea are substantial; and anyone, who, for ten, twenty or thirty years of his life, has devoted two hours a day to such a practice, runs a great risk of resembling the Dormouse or the Hatter. Or again, read the last part of the story, the trial of the Knave of Hearts who had stolen the tarts, as a bit of the *Nursery Rhymes* we have quoted tells us; and among the diverse depositions of the witnesses, each one more extravagant than the others, remember that of Alice:

"What do you know about this business?" the King said to Alice.

"Nothing," said Alice.

"Nothing whatever?" persisted the King.

"Nothing whatever," said Alice.

"That's very important," the King said, turning to the jury. They were just beginning to write this down on their slates, when the White Rabbit interrupted: "Unimportant, Your Majesty means, of course," he said, in a very respectful tone, but frowning and making faces at him as he spoke.

"Unimportant, of course, I meant," the King hastily said, and went on to himself in an undertone, "important — unimportant — unimportant — important," as if he were trying which word sounded best.

Some of the jury wrote it down " important," and some " unimportant."

It is nonsense. But it is not pure invention: there are trials conducted in this way. We laugh for some profound reason of which we are hardly conscious, but which takes shape in our mind. The idea is caricatural, but is not completely false. On the contrary, it touches us by the element of truth that it contains.

The English are a calm and cold people. But let them relax, for a single day, that compulsion for self-control which governs them and they will show a capacity for boisterous unrestraint that is surprising. Let them, for a single day, allow their imagination full swing and they will experiment to the very limits of their repressed curiosity. It is the same with laughter. When they enjoy looking at the universe on its fantastic side, distorting it with deforming mirrors, there is no stopping them. They have their own kind of laughter, rather simple, apparently, but in reality rich with a very complicated content, skillfully mixed with humor. A foreigner can try to understand *Alice in Wonderland;* but to appreciate fully this marvelous story one must be English. An Oxford mathematician, Charles Lutwidge Dodgson, brilliant and shy, ironical and sensitive, preferring the company of children to that of men, made it up one day on the river for a young Alice eager for tales. He published it under the name of Lewis Carroll in 1865. And since then, in the sky of all English children, shine, in a glow of deification, the White Rabbit, the Hatter, the Mock Turtle, and the overbearing Queen of Hearts.

The English are a fearless and strong people. They admire resistant bodies and tenacious wills. Departures, voyages, conquests, distant colonies are their passion. They do not willingly cultivate the soil, but they long to dominate the sea as far as it can carry a vessel.

So their books for children will encourage a taste for sport, and exalt, not the individual triumph, but the victory of the team: that is what counts, and the first condition that this wondeful human machine exacts is voluntary sacrifice and abnegation. Learn, children, to love the sailor's life, set sail in your thoughts, travel over the seas in quest of adventure and danger. Above all, never be afraid. See how the English pull through by means of courage and calm, in shipwrecks and fires, in expeditions against pirates or cannibals, in the land of the yellow or black man. Lost in the desert, prisoners, and already bound to the stake, see, they do not tremble. They know that forceful character is the best remedy for blows of fate, and that after all, it is not so bad a lot to die bravely. *Brave Tales, Bold Ballads and Travels and Perils by Land and Sea* — that is the proper nourishment. *Heroes, Soldiers, Sailors and Travelers* — such must be your models.

Love your country, strive to maintain the strength and grandeur of England. Its absolute superiority over all the other nations of the world is indisputable. This superiority must be considered a dogma established once and for all. You must be its apostles as your fathers, your grandfathers, all your ancestors were. Act; do not waste your time refuting those who contradict you, since no one would do so if he were in his right mind. What were they teaching their children after the wars of the Empire, when the sailors of Trafalgar returned home and were still indignant at the memory of the dangers to which England had been exposed? They were reading *The Youth's Amusement*, which dates from 1818, and found this written under the picture of an armed warrior:

If the French or any other enemy of Great Britain brags about coming among us, of living in our houses, in our country: then let every person able to shoulder a gun come forward as a volunteer, in order to protect his relatives, his property and the government under which he lives.

The young as well as the old were encouraged to volunteer and take up arms. How many challenges, how many bitter remarks were launched in those days against the wicked French, as though they were drawing up plans for an invading army to re-form at Boulogne! Later on, when England, having become the most prosperous and strongest of the European nations, became prideful, what did her newspapers say to children? Listen to this message in the *Young Men of Great Britain*, in 1863:

One can say without boasting that today . . . the name of *Young Men of Great Britain* is a passport to the entire world. Everything that is brave, everything that is generous, everything that is noble and chivalrous in human nature, is expressed in these brief but comprehensive words. Leaving to one side the timid, the persons without ambition, we regard this title as symbolizing the class of audacious and intelligent minds from which have come our Statesmen, our Orators, our Soldiers, our Sailors and our Scientists. From it come the men who make our laws and the men who de-

142

fend our homes. From it come the noble hearts that travel fearlessly over the Seas and that, from one pole to the other, have glorified the name of England.

Coming closer to our own time, when a wave of imperialism passes over her adults, it tries to submerge the children also. *Young Men of Great Britain* is a title that no longer suffices; *Boys of the Empire* translates better the point of view of the country in 1901:

The aim of the journal which will be called *Boys of the Empire* is to support and strengthen the spirit of patriotism and loyalty; and we hope that by means of a league of the whole Empire, we shall accomplish a great and important work uniting in one great comradeship all those who are destined to maintain the glorious tradition of the British race. The members of the *Children's League of the Empire* will not be asked to achieve great sacrifices in time or energy; numerous obligations will not be imposed upon them. We invite them merely to try, through direct and personal effort, to make themselves worthy, from every point of view, of their glorious status as sons of the Empire.

Such are the sentiments that nourished English youth yesterday, day before yesterday, always. And tomorrow what will England be?

To determine that, we can study the color and composition of its ministry, calculate the rate and exchange of the pound, consult all the signs of the present. But let us not overlook the books and newspapers for children! If the English children continue to read and like what Nelson and Wellington read in their youth, England will not change.

What Frenchman, seeking the sources of his love of country, does not include the memory of those books and pictures in which he saw France for the first time? It is like that in every country. The books that, consciously, have exposed to children the glorious annals of the nation are not always those that have had the most influence. Other books, without sacrificing imagination, without wishing to teach anything, have made known the strongest and most subtle qualities inherent in themselves. The elders inculcate in the children the qualities that have made them persevere in their way of life; and no one knows where it begins and no one knows where it will end. The characteristics that make us such-and-such transmit themselves from generation to generation, both by blood and by spirit.

But we must not stop at this point. For children's books repudiate instinctively antagonisms and hatred, mixing indissolubly with a sense of patriotism a sense of humanity.

V

THE SOUL OF MAN

The World Republic of Childhood

WHEN I was a youngster, I remember seeing, in my mind's eye, the whole world spread out before me. One fine day I escaped from my dull town, and with two boys of my own age, André and Julien, traveled all over France through the pages of a beautiful book: Le tour de la France par trois enfants. Another time, led by Don Quixote and Sancho, I saw the plains of Castile, white-hot in the sun, with dusty roads and inns full of adventure. I knew the cork trees and the wild thickets of the Sierra Morena. In my imagination I saw desert isles, the northern lights on the sea. I visited the pigmy country in Africa, which did not seem strange to me as I was familiar with Lilliput. I lived in *Uncle Tom's Cabin* and cultivated sugar cane with black slaves as companions. Like the Baron Munchausen, I fastened a rope to the crescent moon so I could glide to earth, and the rope being too short I cut it above me to at-

tach it to the end which was hanging under my feet.
I went everywhere with Jules Verne, even to the very
bottom of the ocean, and I saw

> . . . the greens, the blues,
> through which, pale, dreaming,
> sometimes a drowned man sinks . . . [1]

Yes, children's books keep alive a sense of nation-
ality; but they also keep alive a sense of humanity.
They describe their native land lovingly, but they
also describe faraway lands where unknown brothers
live. They understand the essential quality of their
own race; but each of them is a messenger that goes
beyond mountains and rivers, beyond the seas, to the
very ends of the world in search of new friendships.
Every country gives and every country receives —
innumerable are the exchanges — and so it comes
about that in our first impressionable years the universal republic of childhood is born.

How many human beings, bound to workbench or
plow, imprisoned in studio or mine, give up reading
after the joyful period of their first leisure is over!
Or else they read newspaper accounts of accidents,
suicides, crimes and wars. How different it was in
their childhood when they used to read books that
the finest writers from all the countries in the world
had written for them. The only rivalry in those days
was in color and picturesque quality. Beautiful stories
grew to completion, doing no harm to one another,
mingling harmoniously. All was peace and unity. If
only their memory could last!

If you look around you when visiting a family, if
you make inquiries in the schools and visit children's

[1] Rimbaud, from "Le Bateau ivre," in *Poésies complètes*, 1895.

libraries, if you note down the names and titles of the child classics, you will see that Germans, English, Americans, Russians, Danes, Swedes, Italians, and French are all the most friendly of neighbors. You may possibly find countries whose people read only foreign books. You will not find a single country that does not admire, even sometimes more than its own best books, books that come from the four quarters of the globe. The world of children is tolerant. It does not know about the prejudices that sometimes can postpone the fame of great books indefinitely. It does not know about wars, how they destroy at a stroke values which once seemed established. It is more loyal than the world of adults which will not hesitate to scorn tomorrow the authors that it praises today, will even pretend to have forgotten their names. Its perception is more alert and more sensitive, since it proceeds not by criticism but by instinct. It stirs up less vanity. Why bother about a writer's origin when it does not mind in the least not knowing the circumstances of his life, or if his nose is short, or if he wears spectacles? " We have Japanese books on our shelves for the children in Boston, our young publishers send people all over the world to hunt stories to translate. Writers from Ireland or Africa, from Italy or Russia settle down in New York."[1]

Smilingly the pleasant books of childhood cross all the frontiers; there is no duty to be paid on inspiration.

Berquin walked about even in Hindustan, dressed in the fashion of that country. *Pinocchio* capers about in America. I have met *Little Red Riding Hood* in Mexico, in Brazil, in the Argentine, in Chili; Ander-

[1] Ernestine Evans, " Trends in Children's Books," *The New Republic,* November 1, 1926.

sen is everywhere. Let us follow *Robinson Crusoe*: the voyages he made while alive are as nothing compared to those he has made since his death. At first he traveled all over England, which was easy; then over the countries where English influence prevailed; so that he has been translated into Arabic, Maori, Bengali, Syrian, Hebrew, Yiddish, Armenian, and Persian. " Finally, since the great Dominions have their own life and literature, the Australian, South African, and Canadian editions of *Robinson Crusoe* have been innumerable, the book having become a classic in all the schools of the world. Thus the genial work of Defoe constantly reminds the English children overseas of the tie which unites them to the tiny land of the Angles lost in the mists to the west of the old continent."[1]

This book reflects England through the courage, the spirit of adventure, the religious quality, the practical character, and even the taste for comfort which it expresses. It is a patriotic book helping to hold together the scattered parts of the great Empire. To make sure we are right about this, let us see what an Englishman, George Borrow, says: " Here is a book that has had a far greater influence on the English mentality than any other of modern times, a book that has been in everybody's hands and whose content is more or less familiar even to those who do not know how to read; a book that has inspired the most exuberant and the most productive of our prose writers; a book to which England owes many of its astonishing discoveries on land and sea and a considerable share of its naval glory."

[1] Paul Dottin, *Daniel Defoe et ses romans*. Paris. Les Presses Universitaires. 1924.

And then *Robinson Crusoe* conquers France where the great voice of Rousseau calls attention to it as the only book suitable for Emile. Its family multiplies like that of a patriarch who has migrated to a fortunate land and before long can hardly count his descendants. The book is so successful in Germany that it creates a literary genre and all through the eighteenth century " Robinsonnades " flourish there. What is more, it takes out naturalization papers and becomes, in 1779, by the medium of Campe's pen, *Robinson der Jüngere*, a German Robinson. In 1813 there comes *The Swiss Family Robinson*, the story of the father who reaches shore in a boat made of tubs, and builds a lodging for his wife and four children in a boabab tree. More or less slowly, but advancing always victoriously, the book conquers Europe, the Latin countries, the Scandinavian, and even the Slav countries which do not entirely understand it but make room for it nevertheless. It conquers South America and its name, way off there, takes on singing inflections, *O Robinson da infancia, El Robinsoncito*.

This book, adopted by the children of every country, is built on an original framework so stout and solid that even under new plastering the ax marks of the old Defoe can always be seen. It is a prodigious performance that never seems to end, each new tide of humanity offering in its turn a fresh version. And what crossbreeding! *The Swiss Family Robinson* and the German Robinson are translated in their turn: " abroad the *Nouveau Robinson* immediately won renown; in the preface of the 7th edition Campe announced with pride that he had not attempted to change a book which had been translated in all the

European languages from Cadiz to Moscow and Constantinople, even in Russian, in modern Greek and in old Czech."[1] This was not vain boasting; before 1800 the *Nouveau Robinson* had already been translated into French, Dutch, Italian, Danish, Greek, Croatian, Czech, and even Latin. In 1853 there appeared an adaptation in Turkish. This German and this Swiss land in England and start new careers in the very country of their forbear. The Swiss borrows some of the features of the German, and in the imitators of the German we find again some features which were borrowed from the Swiss. Madame de Montolieu offers a translation of the original *Swiss Family Robinson* so trim and elegant that she is asked to write a sequel to it and does so, upon which, J. R. Wyss, who wrote the *Swiss Family Robinson*, composes in his turn a series in which he imitates Madame de Montolieu. There are Dutch Robinsons which are translated from the French translation of the English; and others which are translated from German imitations, the Saxon Robinson, the Silesian Robinson, the Brandenburg Robinson. Let us stop there; the genealogical tree of the English hero, son, grandson, great-grandson, nephews, great-nephews, great, great-nephews, relations by marriage and bastards grows higher than the cedar trees, and the children of men are reunited under its branches.

All these fine trees, fortunate enough to survive even though the forest around them perishes, all these famous books that stay eternally young, bear the fruit of peace and scatter seeds of hope. They express understanding of others, acceptance of the unknown,

[1] Paul Dottin. *Daniel Defoe et ses romans*. Paris. Les Presses Universitaires. 1924.

mutual esteem, far-distant friendships that draw hearts and spirits together. *The Wonderful Adventures of Nils* falls into the hands of a bronze-colored child at Singapore or Calcutta. He reads of Nils' travels over Sweden with the wild geese and the many legends and stories Nils heard. He reads the beautiful story of Nils' dream[1] how the Sun traveled towards the North, followed by a procession of beech trees, oaks, lindens, fruits and flowers that advanced joyfully. " Forward! " cries the Sun; " no one needs to be afraid when I am here. Forward! " But several of the travelers hesitate; the roebuck and the wheat stop short at the same moment, and also the blackberry bush, the little yellow buttercup, the chestnut tree and the grouse. The Sun keeps on its way, but it calls and smiles in vain; the ranks thin out to such a point that it would be forsaken by all the animals, plants and men, if new companions were not joining up with it: water willows, white owls, blue foxes, reindeer and Lapps. The Sun scales a mountain that blocks the road and finds itself face to face with the Ice Witch, whose breath brings sleep and death, the aged Troll who wears a snow mantle and whose body is nothing but a piece of ice. The Sun beams and throws forth its rays; the Troll stirs and sighs. But suddenly the Sun utters a cry: " My time is up." It rolls backward; the frigid wind, the cold and the darkness rush after it; it is conquered.

Is not the young Hindu reader amazed by such a story? Strange shapes, unsuspected up to now, ideas which upset everything he knew, enter into his soul to inspire and humanize him. Meanwhile, far away,

[1] *The Further Adventures of Nils,* Chapter XIII, The Dream.

near the borders of Lapland, a child bundled in furs and hugging the fire, reads *The Arabian Nights,* adapted for his enjoyment. He sees airy architecture springing up in the sky, palaces that are mere arabesques, trees with fruits swaying in the soft air, animals that seem unreal to him, horses with finely arched necks and sneering camels, men unlike himself — a whole new world that enters into his soul to exalt and humanize it. Fasten to every book that goes far off into the distant parts of the world one of those invisible threads; they multiply and cross each other in every direction, so that throughout the universe continuously, endlessly, currents of human sympathy flow.

The Brothers Grimm

At the beginning of the nineteenth century in Germany, two brothers were busy with a strange task, so strange that many good souls found it unworthy of serious writers. Scholars, philologists, historians as well as philosophers, Jacob and William Grimm collected tales, much as though they were running after butterflies. As a matter of fact their first thought was to catch the tales while still alive. They went about questioning their men and women friends, asking them to try to remember the stories that had been told to them when they were eight years old; they noted them down immediately. They sought out peasants in the neighborhood of Kassel, their own town, and if they got any sort of a tale from them which seemed to have local color they had the neighbors tell it over again, and if there were any changes, they called these variations and said that they were extremely important.

Through a happy encounter, we made the acquaintance of a Zwelvan peasant woman. We owe it to her that we were able to get some of the tales published here. . . . This woman, still in vigorous health and not much over fifty, is named Viehmännin; she has a strong, pleasant face, with clear, penetrating eyes, and it is quite likely that in her youth she was beautiful. She knows all these old legends by heart, which she says is a gift not granted to everyone. . . . She tells her tales, in a deliberate, assured and animated manner, enjoying the story herself as it flows along. Then if one wishes her to, she repeats it slowly, so that after some training the story can be written under her dictation. Many parts of the tales were preserved in this way, and the truthful quality of the text is unmistakable.[1]

They even talked with servants, begging them to speak in their own dialect, which astonished the good folk no end. People from other provinces sent them tales as they would send gifts. And all this material went to make up the first volume of *Kinder-und Hausmärchen* in 1812. Everybody is familiar with these *Household Stories*.

However, the Grimms had not yet entirely carried out their purpose. For their exalted ideas were more noble than realistic. They wanted to rediscover the poetry of the people which, they said, is the only true poetry, far superior to poetry as an art or to modern poetry, which could never be anything but a clever exercise without ingenuity or genius. True poetry springs from the soul of the nation, and if there is a nation capable of loving, understanding, and preserving it in its purity, that nation is Germany. The nation is inspired by nature, and who inspired nature if not God himself? Poetry, therefore, is of divine

[1] W. Grimm, *Kleinere Schriften,* quoted by E. Tonnelat, *Les Frères Grimm,* Paris, Colin, 1912.

origin. The more humanity withdraws from God (a humanity which is not in progress as the optimists believe, but in decline) the less capable and worthy is it of recreating poetry. The retrieving of the old tales and, in a general sense, of all the notable examples of primitive poetry, means restoring to the national soul its quality of nobility and its harmony with the divine spirit. So the Grimms reasoned it out, point by point, and their reasoning was not always faultless. But if, being romantic and mystic, they wanted to demonstrate the undemonstrable, if they did not prove that in these *Tales* " thoughts concerning the divine and the spiritual have been perpetuated; that ancient faith and religious doctrine have been restored to life by being put into an epic form that develops along with the history of a people," at least the work they did achieve was not in vain.

A taste for folk tales, as savory as home-made bread, that is what children found in their work; that is the superb gift they received from the two German writers. However, as children are not content just to receive, but must give in their turn, often asking favors so they can return them, they have taken it upon themselves to see that this true and sincere portrait of life is placed in a frame of human sympathy. They have made it their business to love it and to make it loved. Let the big leading roles be held for once (so say the children) by woodcutters, plowmen, soldiers returning to their village, farmers' daughters, spinners, artisans, comrades who know their trade so well that one of them is able to shave a hare while running after it, and the other to shoe a galloping horse. Let the big, leading roles be held by lusty fellows who know nothing of fear, and who never manage, in spite of all their efforts, to meet anyone, dead or alive, who can frighten them; by comfortable, placid giants who find it the simplest thing in the world to split a rock with one blow of the fist; Hansel and Gretel, simple babes, as worthy of interest as a king's sons and daughters. As for the kings themselves, they must be kind, just and peace-loving, and keep their word if they want to be liked. From time to time they will be reminded of the equality of man by having to face suffering and death.

We shall make merry at small expense. We shall shout with laughter over the story of the four musicians from Bremen: the tired old ass, the hunting dog whose master wishes him dead, the shabby pussy-cat, the cock with all his feathers gone, who combined their ill luck and started off together for the town where there was a demand for good singers. Clambering up, the dog on the ass, the cat on the dog and the cock on the cat, they appeared all at once at the robbers' window and made such an uproar that the robbers fled and the four cronies had only to seat themselves at the festive board prepared by the fugitives. No longer will they live upon nothing; they will eat heartily, drink without shame, and feel a certain indulgence for that Bavarian peasant who at first begged Heaven for some beer, later on for enough beer to get tipsy, and finally for a cask of beer as an extra. Even the barnyard animals, the hen, the duck, the goat, will receive their share of sympathy. By humbling the proud and exalting the meek the world will move along a little less badly.

In the days when Christ still walked on earth, he knocked at the door of a rich man who refused him a place to rest in his full barns. At last he knocked at the door of a poor man who gave him his bed and provided breakfast for him in the morning. Christ promised to grant the poor man three wishes. The poor man wished for salvation, enough to eat frugally until the end of his days, and, if he should need it, a new house. The rich man, hearing about this, ran after Christ, who promised to grant him likewise his first three wishes. Rich people are not clever, and the bad ones deserve to be punished. So the rich man, in an angry moment, wished that his horse would break its back, which came true. Furious at having to make his way in the sun under the weight of the saddle that he did not want to lose, he wished that his wife, comfortable at that moment in her home, were screwed tight to the saddle forever, which also came true, so that all he had left to wish was that his wife were rid of that cursed saddle and could move about again freely. So he had nothing but bitterness, trouble, hard words, and a dead horse; while the poor man lived a happy, peaceful, and pious life up to a blessed end. The fairy tales of the Grimm Brothers are one of the last places left in the world where we can see the poor get the better of the rich — heroic stronghold defended by the children.

That is their instinct. It never occurs to them that wealth is superior to everything else unless we tell them so. Left to themselves they would have trouble in believing it. There is no little rich boy anywhere, however unpleasant we may imagine him to be, who does not gladly escape from the drawing room to play with those of humbler origin: chauffeurs, mechanics, servants, cooks, mysterious beings, closer to nature and who, as such, hold an invincible attraction for him. There is no little merchant's son who does not make use of his vacation to get closer to the farmer's son, the keeper's son, the fisherman's son. Like Grimm, they go back to the people. It was from them that the children had asked for their first books, in the time of chapbooks and the *Bibliothèque Bleue*. Even persons concerned with writing have something to learn from children. What difference does it make to the youngsters if the style repeats itself sometimes, if it says what it wants to say without too much ceremony? If, instead of worn-out and artificial words, it uses words that are picturesque and genuine? If it is clear? In short, they remind us that the simple forces of the soul, like the simple forces of art, contain the values that endure eternally.

Let us not always seek our human brothers so far away from ourselves. They are very close to us, but we draw ourselves up so tall that we lose them from sight. Take care, the children's books say to us, you are not natural. You are forgetting the virtues of sincerity, innocence, spontaneity. You are going towards artificiality. Happily we are here to remind you that you were born of this earth and that you will again find strength and energy in touching the soil.

Fairy Tales and Their Meaning

Fairy tales are like beautiful mirrors of water, so deep and crystal clear! In their depth we sense the mysterious experience of a thousand years. Their contents date from the primeval ages of humanity, from the fabulous times that Vico tells about when man instinctively created fables and symbols in order to express himself. If you seek to trace the path that a child's story has followed down through the years, if you go back over the course of time trying to find its source, you will often discover that though the story seems new it is very ancient indeed. Scholars will prove to you that it was told in the eighteenth century, even the seventeenth; and that it figured in the inventories that the Renaissance drew up, when it was carefully assembling all the substance of our knowledge. The Renaissance was indebted to the Middle Ages, since it came across the tale in some fable. The Middle Ages had not invented it but taken it from classic antiquity; which in its turn had taken it from the Orient.

You notice, at the same time, that this story multiplies in all the countries, under slightly different forms; that there are Italian, French, Spanish, English, German, and Scandinavian versions of it; that these versions can be arranged in order and in kind; that their essential elements show up in analysis, are well known and have their place in classified folklore. Some attribute this abundant flowering to spontaneous generation and others to infiltration.

What we know is that in these fine tales which delight children, and whose cult is kept alive by them, there are variations that reappear over and over again, and in listening to them, we link ourselves to the most remote members of our race. Once upon a time — yes, once upon a time, formerly, at a period so far removed from us that we are unable to visualize it to ourselves, there was the very same story.

We read again " The Sleeping Beauty." The Prince, after lingering at the home of Beauty and knowing he must explain his tardiness, tells the King, his father, that while hunting he became lost in the forest; that he spent the night in the hut of a charcoal burner, who gave him bread and cheese.

The King, who was a good man, believed him. But his mother was not so easily convinced and, seeing that he went hunting almost every day and that he always had an excuse ready when he spent two or three nights away from home, suspected a romance. Indeed, he lived with the Princess for more than two whole years and had two children; the first, being a girl, was named Dawn, and the second, a boy, was named Day, because he was still more beautiful than his sister. Several times the Queen told her son, hoping to draw him out, that we must try to be happy in life, but he never dared confide his secret to her. He feared her although he loved her, for she had ogress blood in her and the King had wed her only because of her material possessions. It was even whispered about in court that she had the inclinations of an ogre and when she saw little children passing by had all the trouble in the world to keep herself from seizing them. So naturally the Prince did not want to say anything.

The awakening of this Beauty, asleep for so long a time, can it be the awakening of Nature at the call of Spring? The Ogress who wants to devour Dawn and Day, could that be Night? Or have these personages escaped from the festivities of Carnival, to find eternal refuge in the tales? While we watch Dwarfs and Giants at play, are we feeling again the amazement of primitive man gazing at the wonders of creation in the infinitely big and the infinitely small? When we witness the struggles between the good fairies and the wicked magicians, are we witnessing also, in this primitive and ancestral form, the eternal struggle between Good and Evil, Life and Death? We are not concerned here with the problem of the origin of fables, but even the uninitiated, however little they may think about it, sense that they are filled with a long, human past.

In the Nursery Rhymes that children repeat, in England, in Germany, and which they keep alive from generation to generation, there are not only fragments of history, but there are, behind and beyond the reach of history, the echoes of rites infinitely far off, rites which were performed in marriage, baptism or death; Christian customs, pagan customs, customs which were alive so many centuries ago that we hardly dare surmise the date, in civilizations that have disappeared. In these tales that so many people may find rather silly can be found, so wise men tell us, an entire poetic mythology, a reflection of the first dawn of human imagination. Hearing these tales, each one of which conceals a chaotic mixture of a thousand themes, sometimes inextricable, we return to a time when the beasts and the plants talked; when the soul left the body during the night and sought its own innumerable adventures; when it hid itself in a flower, in a tree, in an animal of the forest or plain; when it became smoke, shadow, mirror. Sorcerers again assert their magic power; with a wave of their wand they can work wonders. With an incantation they can transform strength into weakness, weakness into strength, or bring the dead to life. Pleasures become again those of the body, accustomed to hardship which must win its daily bread and the right to rest after incessant struggle: tables laden with food, cups always full, sleep rich with happy dreams. Nature is again filled with Phantoms, helpful or cruel, and strangely powerful, the longed-for Day and the frightening Night, the Sun and the Moon and the stars in the heavens.[1]

[1] See H. L. Koester, *Geschichte der deutschen Jugendliteratur*, 4. Auflage, 1927.

Perhaps they wish to draw us still farther back, to the awakening of an undefined soul, unable to distinguish the ego from the non-ego, to separate reality from dream? Let us yield to the impulse which leads us, by way of the tales, back to those remote regions which even imagination itself has trouble in reaching. See how every child repeats, through the tales, the history of our species and takes up anew the journey of our spirit from its beginnings. Threats, pursuit, mountains that cannot be climbed, rivers that cannot be crossed, all this dream material is found again in the fabulous stories that please little children. Like themselves, in the life that they begin and to which they return as soon as they fall asleep, their favorite heroes soar, glide, fly, cover seven leagues at one stride. The impossible and the possible mingle. The conscious does not differ from the subconscious. The universe is not yet organized according to the laws of reason, but the individual is aware of it in each of its manifestations. It is the individual himself. Matter is alive; everything is real, nothing is real. And this chaos, far from astonishing a child reader, seems natural to him, as if he remembered passing through it himself some twenty thousand years ago.

Peter Pan

Sometimes the soul of man needs to be protected against itself to prevent it from changing everything it touches into hard gold. It needs to have reserved for it some regions that are not under cultivation. Like the forests in America that are saved from an invasion of dwellings and factories, it needs to be kept young, and sheltered from disease as long as possible.

New heroes are still being welcomed on the miniature Olympus where Man Friday, Gribouille, Schneewittchen, Pinocchio, General Dourakine and other illustrious shades do nothing now but drink ambrosia, and where horses and asses, Rozinante, Platero, Cadichon, graze eternally. The newest of them is called Peter Pan. Christmas brought him, for he appeared for the first time on a London stage, the 26th of December, 1904. Christmas saw him reappear for many years in London, Edinburgh, Glasgow, Dublin, in the country towns, in every town where he could make himself understood without a translator, and soon even in the others. Christmas is a fine season for dreaming.

The curtain goes up. Everyday life gives way to a second kind of reality incomparably finer. Twinkling lights, settings, ballets, songs, cause one to forget the mud and rain outside. As though under a charm, the spectators begin a beautiful dream. They follow Peter Pan, Peter Pan who found a way of never growing up and of keeping his body and soul like a child's. One evening he vanished from home and as there was no nursemaid or policeman or any kind of adult to hold him back, he made straight for Kensington Gardens, towards the trees whose tops he had seen swaying. Oh, if men could only fly away like Peter Pan, fly away to gardens that would become their home forever! They would no longer belong entirely to their own wretched species. They would be " Betwixt and Between," intermediaries between reality and dream. They would inhabit a secret isle in the middle of the Serpentine lake where they would have only the birds for company. The birds would help them build a floating nest so they could cross the river and at night go on excursions to the other side of the water. But in the daytime they would come back to their isle, a cosy place to hide in. No longer would wickedness, or self-interest, or jealousy come near them. They would talk with old Solomon, the wise and serious crow. They would hear the language of the magpies, blackbirds and other Lords and Ladies who would not consider them entirely their equals, but who would forgive them for taking food with their hands instead of their beaks as is proper, for birds are tolerant and even charitable. They would be engrossed all day long and even busy, busy doing nothing. They would make reed pipes and amuse themselves imitating the sound of the wind in the leaves, the sound of insects quivering in the grass, the sound of frogs jumping into the water. Sometimes in the evening from their rustic flute would seem to come forth the voice of the nightingale.

They would come to know the fairies, real fairies, not the kind usually depicted by those who have not kept company with them often enough, but real fairies who exist only for the pleasure of living and peopling the earth. Fairies as heedless, whimsical, easily startled as rabbits that hop about and dart into their burrows; light heads, tiny hearts, in which there is room, however, for kindness, for gratitude; delicate bodies that are mistaken for flowers, but not entirely mistaken since they really are both flowers and fairies. At night, when the garden gates are closed, and they are sure of not being disturbed, their fetes begin. While the trees, tired of standing still in their places, walk about talking with each other, the fairies go to their parties, chattering, flitting about, dancing to the music of Peter Pan's pipes.

Peter Pan has not become a creature without consciousness. He has the privilege of loving, of suffering like all created beings. The fairy flowers themselves are familiar with suffering and love. There are flowers with hard hearts, disdainful of those who adore them, that all at once begin to be loving, nobody knows why. But his feelings are blurred, hazy, intermittent, as is natural for a Between. The keenest sorrow he feels is nostalgia, nothing seems unbearable, neither the longings of his heart nor the certainty that they will not be fulfilled. He is gay without noisy outbursts or loud laughter. One day he steals away to his old home and, looking through the window, sees that his mother has consoled herself for his departure with another child. He would be in despair, if despair did not seem to evaporate in the mist when he reached his isle again. He is disappointed; he is mildly sad. So it is with pleasures.

Along the garden paths he chances on Maimie, the daring little girl who wanted to spend a night in Kensington Gardens and to accomplish it escaped from her nurse at the very moment the gates were to be closed. Peter Pan is not familiar with little girls, but he discovers that Maimie is as soft as a bird's nest. He is happy to have her consider him good, courageous, and strong. He is enraptured to touch his lips to her cheek. He would like to have this little creature, dropped from the sky, climb into his boat made of straw and feathers, and cross the Serpentine. He would like to carry her off to the inaccessible isle, where she would consent to stay with him, forgetful of her mother, her brother and her home. Alas! Maimie, about to listen to him, and already on the shore of the isle, escapes at the sound of the gates reopening and to console Peter Pan promises to return the following night. Peter Pan waits for her but Maimie does not return.[1]

Men come to the performance given by Peter Pan to dream, pretending that they have come to bring their children who have been good. They seek a pretext to excuse themselves. Just as, taken by surprise reading stories not meant for grownups, they declare they had nothing else at hand or that they ought to know the kind of thing their sons and daughters are enjoying.

They would do better to spare their pretexts, not to blush, but to set out eagerly to those fortunate isles where they will find freshness and youth. The books that have told the fine story over and over again, so that everyone knows it, say that Peter Pan is always in Kensington Gardens. He spends his nights riding about perched on a goat that the fairies gave him at Maimie's wish; an enchanting music comes forth from his reed pipes. Or he may be lying on the grass, waving his small feet in the air, happy as can be. He leads a life that is good to live with his boat, pipes, goat, and fairies. And the best of it is that it will go on forever, for Peter Pan will never grow up. Those who, passing by the gates of the big garden and remembering his existence, try to catch the sound of the sweet, nocturnal tune so like the nightingale's, if they succeed in hearing it, will be saved from growing old for a long, long time.

[1] *Peter Pan in Kensington Gardens,* by J. M. Barrie.

The World as Seen by Children

Children lead us back to the fountainhead. We are blasé; we have seen too many strange things. They call, inviting us to look at, and admire, pictures that owe their strength to their simplicity. I do not mean only those conjured up by the printer's type, but those set down on the pages in bold lines, with plenty of color. A whole group of illustrators has placed itself at their service, from Thomas Bewick, who engraved on wood the animals that run over the earth or that fly the heavens, to Rackham, who perpetuates in his drawings and paintings the secret of their soul, so complicated, ingenuous and tender. I have sympathy for those inquiring minds, attracted by new ideas, who, exasperated by the banal, resort to riot and revolution to drive it away. But it is sweet sometimes, I admit, to see the world again with a child's eyes.

It is true that they lure us away from the feast of ideas, taking no pleasure there themselves. They place small value on the abstractions that are so useful to our grown-up pastimes. No doubt it sometimes happens that the stories most laden with meaning seem easy for them to take hold of, as though they had already lived several lives, the confused memory of which survives; or as if they had foreknowledge of their own completion; or as if intuition accomplished its miracle in them and allowed them to reach their goal while sparing them the journey to it. But these are only exceptional rays of light. Let us not exaggerate, let us not grant them every quality, let us admit that they have no skill in handling ideas. What they have is enough for them.

There is a freshness in their way of feeling. There

is no savoring of gloom, no perversity. Childhood does not understand the pleasure there is in being sad, or holding on to grief so as to relish it slowly. It remains healthy because it has not yet reached the age for analyzing the soul's emotions, for observing each of its impressions to see how it may develop, following with curiosity the extension of the emotional life beyond good and evil. We have noticed that children want writers to believe in the reality of the external world, to be interested in things for what they are and not to gauge the sensations that they receive from them. They have no use for dilettantes or skeptics. Who can deny that everyone who comes into the world brings with him his own share of egoism? We wonder how we have ever been able to believe and uphold that men are born naturally good. Children are not proud of their egoism. They are incapable of raising it to a system, to a rule of conduct. To disguise it as egotism — that is a grown-up invention and not of their doing. The same instinct that carries them towards life carries them towards the values which give a meaning to this life, towards moral values, towards social values, which, through time-honored experience, have proved to be the best guardians.

The primeval gestures of human affection, the desire to be together, the devoted watchfulness, compassion, gentleness and brotherly confidence develop in the warm atmosphere of a happy family life. Up to the age of twelve years, the sentiments that influence a child are those which concern his idea of himself or his own safety and well-being. He feels in himself the generosity he needs, the courage and honor that complement his innate fear and desire for praise, the faithfulness and devotion natural to his unavoidable dependence, the family sentiments that satisfy his interests and his instincts for veneration, the respect, the love of justice that his lack of strength arouses, the love of liberty that his experience and discipline awaken in him.[1]

Girls demand books that demonstrate maternal feelings in action. Their sympathy is won by heroines who are kind to the afflicted, charitable to the poor, devoted to the sick; by those who take up bravely the daily tasks of the household so as to provide for the loved ones not only the security of affection, but well-being, material comfort, a happy life: both Martha and Mary. Boys demand books of valor, where cowards make a poor showing, where liars are unmasked and punished, and the vainglorious are derided; stories of generous rivalries, where the best man wins; adventures and vicissitudes which exalt the human and increase his strength. Boys and girls want books where truth and justice triumph in the end. The bandit may be a sympathetic character but the police must win out — unless we are able to invent a particularly delightful and virtuous bandit. Boys and girls do not object to quarrels, provided they end with handshakes or an embrace; misfortunes, provided they turn into luck. They do not like self-pity or ill-fated women who never manage to get cheered up, or gloomy dramas. On the contrary: "They married, they were happy and had lots of children."

Boys and girls demand, in no uncertain terms, to be told about modern inventions. They almost scorn people who still go about in automobiles instead of airplanes. Daring and success in human affairs do not seem at all paradoxical and remarkable, but natu-

[1] Scheid, *L'Evolution du sens littéraire chez l'enfant* (Revue pédagogique, janvier 1912).

ral and desirable. Children traveled, without aston-
ishment, twenty thousand leagues under the sea long
before there were any submarines. We belong to an
old civilization, and it was not merely yesterday that
we were calling ourselves decadent. Our taste is weary;
it has to have refined and complicated dishes to stimulate it. We admire, in spite of ourselves, books whose
authors have descended into the depths of the soul,
and brought us back strange flowerings. Let us think
gratefully of those who, through children and for
children, perform the miracle of springtime; of those
who, like Andersen, rediscover the blessings of charm,
freshness, and candor; a breath of pure air to inspire
each new generation. " There is, near here," said the
Beautiful Maiden with golden hair, in a fairy tale, " a
deep cavern which is all of six leagues in circumfer-
ence. There are two dragons at the entrance to prevent anyone from entering. There is fire in their
jaws and eyes. Then, once inside the cavern, there is a
great hole to descend. It is full of snakes, toads and
serpents. At the bottom of this hole there is a tiny cel-
lar where the fountain of beauty and health flows. It
is some of that water that I must have. Everything
that is washed with it becomes miraculous."

Many of the stories that please little children are
love stories. How a monster dared to idolize the most
beautiful of women, and proved himself to be so
humble, so helpful, and so stubbornly in love with
her, that she ended by idolizing him. How a prince,
in order to remain faithful to his princess, suffered
himself to be changed into a bluebird. How little
Gerda followed Kay, without whom she could not
live, to the very palace of the Snow Queen. How the
little mermaid, having loved the son of an earthly

king, through her love found death and, later on, immortality. What do they know of love? Nothing, like Peter Pan. But they have a presentiment of it in its noblest and highest form: an aspiration that delights in sacrifice, a harmony preordained, against which no oppression shall avail, a desire for perfection, ideal strength, the salvation of the world. Plato, in saying that love is an entirely spiritual principle: the impulse of two souls who seek one another in order to form a perfect whole, the symbol of supreme unity, would not astonish a little child.

Heroes

How would heroism be kept alive in our aging earth if not by each fresh, young generation that begins anew the epic of the human race? The finest and noblest of the books intended for children tell of heroism. They are the inspiration of those who, later in life, sacrifice themselves that they may secure safety for others.

Charles Kingsley wrote a book for his own children, Rose, Maurice, and Mary, and called it *Heroes*. He drew his characters from the Greek epic and they stand out in his book, bathed in the clear light of the Mediterranean, as though they were living statues of humanity's benefactors. He told the story of Jason, who won the Golden Fleece after running enormous risks that would have terrified any heart less sturdy; of Theseus, who killed the monsters that laid waste the land of Hellas, who fearlessly attacked the Minotaur and vanquished it; of Perseus who delivered both the land and the sky from Medusa the Gorgon. Perseus was so handsome that he was called the son of

Zeus. At the age of fifteen he was a head taller than all the men of his isle. Perseus was the best at wrestling, at racing, at throwing the javelin. Before risking his life in a great enterprise, he fortified himself in soul and body. For a hero does not follow the well-worn path of those who are easily satisfied or discouraged, nor does he believe he has fulfilled his whole duty when he has sacrificed lambs to the Divinity. He must offer himself. One day Pallas Athena appeared before him:

I am Pallas Athena; and I know the thoughts of all men's hearts, and discern their manhood or their baseness. And from the souls of clay I turn away, and they are blessed but not by me. They fatten at ease, like sheep in the pasture, and eat what they did not sow, like oxen in the stall. They grow and spread, like the gourd along the ground; but like the gourd, they give no shade to the traveler, and when they are ripe death gathers them, and they go down unloved into hell, and their name vanishes out of the land.

But to the souls of fire I give more fire, and to those who are manful I give a might more than man's. These are the heroes, the sons of the Immortals, who are blest, but not like the souls of clay. For I drive them forth by strange paths, Perseus, that they may fight the Titans and the monsters, the enemies of Gods and men. Through doubt and need, danger and battle, I drive them; and some of them are slain in the flower of youth, no man knows when or where; and some of them win noble names, and a fair and green old age; but what will be their latter end I know not, and none knows, save Zeus, the father of Gods and men. Tell me now, Perseus, which of these two sorts of men seem to you more blest?

Perseus does not wish to be like the cattle that fatten in the meadow; Perseus does not wish death to take him before he has won glory and love. He flies over the sea with his winged sandals, his invincible sword, his shield in which the face of the Gorgon will be reflected. He strikes down the monster. He gives thanks to the Gods, as heroes should do, since without the Gods there is no strength or wisdom. He reigns peacefully over Argus, accomplishing the most difficult task of all, which is to remain true to himself, with spirit resolute and without arrogance, after winning his victory. Then he dies, or at least he seems to die. For in the daytime he stands on the lofty peaks which project beyond the clouds and where the winds themselves no longer blow, in company with the Immortals. At evening he becomes a star; all through the night he can be seen shining in the sky, to guide the sailors who have lost their way.

APPENDIX

TRANSLATOR'S NOTE

I
N 1933, Esther Averill sent to Boston, from Paris, a box of recent French books, selected by her with her usual flair for material of permanent value. These books were to be sold at The Bookshop for Boys and Girls where Bertha Mahony was building up a choice stock of children's books in foreign languages, sensing that in the days ahead we were all to become more internationally literate. One of the books in the box was *about* children's books, *Les Livres, les Enfants et les Hommes,* by Professor Paul Hazard.

This book proved to be so fascinating in its contents, so valuable for its scholarly richness, for its appeal to anyone interested in the combination of child and book, that an English translation seemed a desirable step towards bringing Paul Hazard's work the recognition it should have in this country where the author has for many years been a beloved and honored visitor. In his own country his knowledge of history and comparative literature has been an inspiration to innumerable young European writers who have studied under him.

Paul Hazard was born in 1878 in a small village called Nordpéene, close to the Belgian frontier. In 1903 he completed his work at the famous *Ecole Normale Supérieure* in Paris. He became *Docteur-es-Lettres* in 1910 and began to teach Comparative Literature at Lyons University. After three years at Lyons he was invited to come back to Paris to the Faculty of the Sorbonne, and in 1925 was appointed to the chair of Modern Literature in the *Collège de France*. He is an Associate Member of the Royal Academy of Belgium. He received the Doctor of Laws degree from Harvard in 1936 and the degree of Doctor of Letters from Columbia in 1940. He became a member of the French Academy in 1940, filling the chair left vacant by the death of Georges Goyau.

Many literati, in France and elsewhere, do all their traveling in books; they rarely bestir themselves and move beyond their own frontiers. But Paul Hazard was not satisfied to obtain his knowledge of other peoples entirely from books. He went to South America, to the United States, to Spain, to Denmark, to England, to Italy. In *Quand un Flamand découvre l'Italie,* a short article in *Les Nouvelles Littéraires,* written in 1940, he tells of the joyous months he spent in Italy as a young man, discovering the Italy of those happier days: " The air was purer, the sun brighter, the future more full of promise, and we worked gaily to attain, in some definite sense, the universal brotherhood of man." In the first world war it was a great satisfaction to him to be able to serve as liaison officer with the Italian army. He was awarded the Croix de Guerre. His book *Italie Vivante,* according to Victor Giraud, is one of the most suggestive volumes that had been written about Italy before the second world war.

When Joseph Bédier was asked by Larousse to compile *L'Histoire de la Littérature Française,* he invited Paul Hazard, who had been one of his favorite pupils, to collaborate with him. The two large volumes resulting from their work together appeared in 1924 and are now famous.

In 1935 Paul Hazard wrote his *Crise de la Con-*

science Européenne in three volumes, considered by many scholars to be one of the most brilliant literary accomplishments of our generation.

Unable to accept an appointment as visiting Professor of French at Columbia University in 1914 because of the outbreak of the first world war, he did not come over here regularly in that capacity until 1932, but continued from then on to come for one semester every other year until 1941, when he decided he must return to France. He sailed for that country in January, 1941. Horatio Smith of the French Department at Columbia wrote in a letter: " We tried to persuade him to stay at Columbia and wanted him to remain here as a regular member of our staff, but he felt that it was his duty to return to his country in its distress and no arguments about the service he could render to his country here seemed valid enough to him to hold him.

"After his return he was named Rector of the University of Paris, but the Nazis would have none of him and he never actually took the post. He taught at Lyons through the first part of 1941, and then returned to Paris as Professor at the *Collège de France* near the end of the summer of 1941. I have had a few communications from him since his return to France, the most recent being a letter dated September 6, 1942, which he was able to send me from what was then the free zone of France where he was making a brief visit. It was then his plan to return to Paris and to the *Collège de France*. As to his recent situation, I can only affirm that he tells me that his health is good and it is clear that his spirit is indomitable."

Perhaps the following quotation from an article that Paul Hazard wrote in *La Revue des Deux Mondes* in 1939, entitled "*Au Pays de la Jeunesse*," will make it clearer to us all why he felt so deeply in 1941 that he must be back among those young students whom he had taught so wisely and loved so understandingly.

"When I read in any foreign newspaper," wrote Paul Hazard, "the announcement of our decadence and the notice of our death, I laugh to myself at this false prophet, thinking of the surprise that the near future is preparing for him. Those people who are in such a hurry to have us disappear off the world's map, have they no ears to hear, no eyes to see? They should watch our students at the Sorbonne and talk with them. They should see with what courage these young people face the endless examinations we load upon them! With what serenity this generation born to danger gets on with its daily tasks! What an appetite it has not only for ideas but for action! The reviews in which our future men of letters, our future statesmen express their desires and trends are no less significant. No longer are they called the *Revue Indépendante* or *Vogue* or *Décadent*; they are called *Civilisation, Culture, Esprit, Volontés. . . .*"

M. M.

April 2, 1943

PAUL HAZARD

ON the morning of April 16, 1944, I read a review of *Books, Children and Men* in the *New York Times* and took pleasure in the discernment of the reviewer, who although he certainly did not know Paul Hazard personally sensed through the book the author's charm and wisdom. On that same Sunday afternoon news came to the New York O. W. I., and in short-wave broadcasts from Paris and Berlin, that Paul Hazard was dead. I did not dare not believe it. Hazard was not after all a political personage and there would seem to be no motive in spreading false reports. He was sixty-six years old — which I would not be willing to consider even senescent for him in any ordinary circumstances; but since 1940 he had had tragic experiences, in terms of the country he loved so intensely, and he had been physically tried by an attack of pneumonia suffered two years ago at his little country house near Gisors, in the winter, without warmth or drugs or doctor. He had described this situation to me in one of his last letters, before the total occupation of France by the enemy, and referred in the simplest and bravest of words to slow and difficult recovery. Such an illness might well have undermined permanently the health of the most robust of men. This summer confirming word has come from a disciple of Hazard in Switzerland, by way of England, that he has indeed died.

At the very beginning of the war Hazard, with the

rank of Lieutenant-Colonel, was attached to the French Information Service, where his understanding of foreign languages and cultures and psychologies, and his talents as a writer could be made to render their maximum of usefulness.

He could love and he could hate and he was able to convey both emotions to his readers on a plane worthy of Robert Frost's poem about fire and ice. I have here in my Vermont study the scathing article he wrote against the Nazis and on behalf of Paris in *Le Temps* for June 8, 1940. Entitled " Frenzy " (" *Délire* "), on the subject of the lies of the Nazis, it is addressed to all lovers of France. It begins:

Friends abroad, I do not know what German propaganda may be concocting for your ears, but I do know what it is telling us, and however insensible I may have become to the idiocy and perfidy of its inventions, I perceive that at this moment it is surpassing itself.

It is informing us that disorder and terror reign inside of Paris. And never has Paris been more calm, more noble, more lovely! Her springtime robe is immaculate; the great city is like a beehive where everyone is completely occupied with his own regularly assigned task; the places for pleasure are closed but the places for work are open day and night. If you should go into her churches, Saint Etienne du Mont, Notre Dame, you would hear the prayers that are lifted to Saint Genevieve, to Joan of Arc, to the God of Justice and Truth.

The same number of *Le Temps* had a leading editorial entitled " Hold Firm " (" *Tenir* "). We know that a few days later human flesh and human spirit had to yield for the time to machines and brute force.

Hazard was ordered to Bordeaux, and then came the armistice and the end of any opportunity of immediate official service. He started for Lisbon, and eventually New York, where he was scheduled to resume his duties as Professor of French Literature at Columbia University for another semester. A French scholar does not willingly, perhaps I should say could not conceivably, relinquish the business of being a scholar. We heard he was on his way; Columbia friends greeted him and Mme. Hazard at the pier and one of these, a compatriot and a disciple, Jean-Albert Bédé, gave him my invitation. Would they spend the summer with us in Vermont? We wanted them ardently, and they finally promised to join us, after some Gallic reticence, " *discrétion*," about any possibility of intruding, even upon my family which had so often been their guests in France.

Once persuaded they accepted with French reasonableness the consequences of the decision, came, settled in, and were definitely and at once members of our household. Not without some shocks, especially as to the surroundings, I suspect, although these were kept under control. Neither Paul nor Alice Hazard had had any experience with truly rural America; they knew New York and Boston and Chicago. We are sixteen miles from the railway, on a road that now merges with the wilderness a little farther on, although it retains the dignity of having served Stark to get to Bennington a century and a half ago. The route which I took for bringing them to the farm is through miles and miles of national forest, no human habitation is visible from my hillside, and nothing is audible except the birds. The contrast was violent, after the tumult and the devastation they had seen, but a sudden application of peace and quiet was what the dear nerve-frayed pair needed more than anything else in the world. They adjusted, as I say, with decision — also with grace. We talked of the war when they wished to, and they surely never got it out of their minds and hearts, but it was not often on their lips. Vermont is a good place for the exchange of silences.

Vermont was a revelation to Hazard, and, as the French say, " Reciprocally." For Hazard was a revelation to this corner of New England. We have some very genuine Vermonters about us, and occasionally working for us and even honoring us with a call. One of them was a sort of semi-demi-hired man that summer and regularly devoted one full day a week to us; in September, when I said to him jokingly that he was going to miss us, it was he who in the same vein and in full and adequate simplicity retorted, " Fridays." It was fascinating to see how Hazard, though English was not his major foreign language, relished such Vermont succinctness, and aroused and returned Vermont friendliness. Hazard was even once convinced that the same semi-demi-hired man was making a commendable effort to speak French when one day, asked if he would like a drink with us, the answer of our neighbor was " Maybe." This was taken for "*Mais oui,*" until we pointed out, reluctantly, that it was the purest " vermontois." Hazard was delighted to discover in these hills characters comparable to the stalwart French *paysan* he knew so well, and a native culture as deep-rooted and as fine. The people here sensed his own quality. One of my neighbors proved susceptible to the point of appearing on August 14, the last morning of the year for trout, and spreading out on the grass before us, as a delicacy for our French guests, all of his final picturesque catch. I can still see the flashing of the speckled brook trout and the gleam in Hazard's eye as he realized that our own Paul liked him and knew he had been through deep trouble and was offering what he could in the way of a friendly and authentically local gesture.

The country itself Hazard thought lovely, as indeed it is, but I must confess he was more interested in the people. He remained the student of humanity. We have seen his imaginative and subtle comprehension of young human nature in *Books, Children and Men*. I had known how gracious and successful a host he could be to children in the case of my own, whom he once entertained at Gisors, showing them just enough of the old town to amuse them without strain and then heading straight for the best *pâtisserie*. He had the same gift for understanding his students, and it is no wonder that his disciples are legion. Nothing human was alien to this descendant of Rome — and Greece — and Vermont was full of new material.

At the same time he was incorrigibly a man of letters. It is characteristic that the title of the present work begins with "Books." Of course, he had to have books that summer. We called upon the resources of the university library and he settled down in my study to complete the preparation of the course he was to give for us that fall. Indeed, once installed in this room, which had been the kitchen in the oldest part of the house and was now lined with the gray boards that had had a hundred years of Vermont weathering on its outside — once installed here and especially before the open fire which we frequently needed, I had difficulty in getting him to move. He would on occasion yield to a particularly radiant afternoon, but for the most part he wanted to dedicate the days — and I never tired of attacking him as a French intellectual — to the volumes in which he was investigating the ideas on *nature* of eighteenth-century France. I nearly yielded myself to the temptation to stay always at the other table in the study, where I had my books on Montaigne, partly because I had serious business with Montaigne and partly because he often needed to feel that a friend was near and partly because it is not every day — and this time it *was* every day — that an American teacher of French has a Member of the French Academy within ten feet for all inquiries. How we did multiply questions, and discussions!

The summer had to come to an end and the Hazards had to go back to the city and we had soon to follow. Their last day they went down the ravine to our brook, which they called " *le torrent* " and which is most certainly that after a storm, and which being also spring-fed maintains forever its own activity — they went down to " *le torrent* " and both drank of its waters, as a symbol for their coming back.

Paul never will. The following semester he was again the eloquent and masterful teacher and scholar we knew and then he went back to France. We tried to persuade him that he could do little at that time in France in its enslavement and that no other Frenchman could be so noble a representative of the permanent qualities of his own country at a period when such representation was greatly needed by France in the United States. He never agreed. As matters had resolved themselves in France he felt that he must be there at the scheduled date to continue, according to whatever possibilities, the work of a Professor of the *Collège de France*. Above all he was determined to share, in immediate contact with his fellow-countrymen, the hardships, physical and spiritual, it was clear were to be for a time their daily lot. And so he went, with Alice Hazard who could not have conceived of letting him depart alone. He wrote us with such regularity as was possible until the North African campaign and the total occupation of his own country. We know that he taught at the *Collège de France* as transferred from Paris to Lyons, that his government proposed him for the Rectorship of the University of Paris and that the Nazis to his great honor would have none of him, that he later continued his lectures at the *Collège de France* in Paris.

I had been keeping his author's copies of the American edition of *Books, Children and Men* for delivery to him after the war, and know with what delight he would have seen the worthy printing and format and the no less worthy and altogether admirable translation. I am at this moment in the chair he occupied in this one-time Vermont kitchen and I look at these hills which did bring him strength in time of trouble, and if I listen intently I can hear what I think of as his brook. He left his stamp here as in all that he did and all that he wrote.

HORATIO SMITH

Londonderry, Vermont
August 1, 1944

BIBLIOGRAPHY

BOOK I

G. Fanciulli, E. Monaci, *La letteratura per l'infanzia.* Società editrice internazionale, Torino (1926).

H. L. Koester, *Geschichte der deutschen Jugendliteratur.* Braunschweig, Berlin, Hamburg, G. Westermann, 1927 (4e Auflage).

M. Labry-Hollebecque, *Les Origines de la littérature enfantine (Cahiers de l'Etoile,* troisième année, n° 17, septembre-octobre 1930).

C. Burnite, *The Beginning of a Literature for Children (The Library Journal,* 1906).

M. T. Latzarus, *La littérature enfantine en France dans la seconde moitié du dix-neuvième siècle.* Paris, Presses Universitaires, 1923.

Mary-Elizabeth Storer, *La mode des Contes de fées* (1635-1700). Paris, Champion, 1928.

André Hallays, *Les Perrault.* Paris, Perrin, 1926.

Jeanne Roche-Mazon, *En marge de l'Oiseau Bleu (Cahiers de la Quinzaine,* dix-septième cahier de la dix-neuvième série, 1930).

Jean Harmand, *Madame de Genlis. Sa vie intime et politique,* 1746-1830. Paris, Perrin, 1912.

Andrew W. Tuer, *History of the Hornbook.* London, The Ledenhall Press, 1897.

John Ashton, *The Chapbook of the Eighteenth Century.* London, Chatto and Windus, 1882.

Charles Welsh, *A Bookseller of the Last Century.* Printed for Griffith, Farran, Okeden and Welsh, successors to

Newbery and Harris, at the Sign of the Bible and Sun, West Corner of St. Paul's Churchyard, London; and E. P. Dutton and Co., New York, 1885.

CONSTANCE HILL, *Maria Edgeworth, and Her Circle in the Days of Buonaparte and Bourbons*. London, John Lane; New York, John Lane Co., 1909.

GESIENA ANDRECE, *The Dawn of Juvenile Literature in England*, Amsterdam, H. J., Paris, 1925.

A. C. MOORE, *Roads to Childhood*. New York, G. H. Doran, 1920.

La Nouvelle Education, revue mensuelle, 1921-1931.

BOOK II

ANATOLE FRANCE, *Le livre de mon ami*. Paris.

PAUL DOTTIN, *Daniel Defoe et ses romans*. Paris, Les Presses Universitaires, 1924.

EMILE PONS, *La jeunesse de Swift et le Conte du Tonneau*. Strasbourg, Imprimerie alsacienne, 1925.

S. GOULDING, *Swift en France au dix-huitième siècle*. Paris, Champion, 1924.

C. M. HEWINS, *Books for the Young*. New York, Leypoldt, 1883.

CHARLES WELSH, *Children's Books That Have Lived* (in *The Library. A quarterly review of bibliography* . . . New series, vol. I, London, 1900 and *The Library Journal*, vol. 27, 1902).

C. M. HEWINS, *Report on Lists of Children's Books With Children's Annotations* (*Library Journal*, vol. 27, 1902).

W. C. BERWICK SAYERS, *The Children's Library*, London, Routledge, 1912.

ARTHUR GROOM, *Writing for Children. A Manual of Juvenile Fiction*. London, A. and C. Black, 1929.

A. Dupuy, *Un personnage nouveau du roman français: l'enfant*. Paris, Hachette, 1930.

Calvet, Abbé J., *L'enfant dans la littérature française*. Paris, Lanore, 1932, 2 vol.

BOOK III

Children's Books in the United States, Prepared for the World Federation of Education Associations. Chicago, American Library Association, 1929.

Children's Library Yearbook, Number Two. Chicago, American Library Association, 1930.

Children's Books from Twelve Countries. Chicago, American Library Association, 1930.

Bertha E. Mahony and Elinor Whitney, *Realms of Gold in Children's Books*. New York, Doubleday, Doran and Co., 1929.

Floris Delattre, *La littérature enfantine en Angleterre* (*Revue pédagogique*, 15 août 1907).

C. Burnite, *The Beginnings of a Literature for Children* (*The Library Journal*, 1906).

Katherine Elwes Thomas, *The Real Personages of Mother Goose*. Boston, Lothrop, 1930.

P. Lelièvre, *John Bunyan et le Voyage du Pèlerin*. Paris, 1896.

Charles Schmidt, *Bibliothèques pour enfants* (*Revue de Paris*, 1er juin 1931).

Madeleine Cazamian, *L'autre Amérique*. Paris, Champion, 1931.

Marcelle Tinayre, *Introduction à Hans Christian Andersen. Contes choisis*. Traduction et notes par Pierre Mélèze. Paris, La Renaissance du livre.

André Balsen, *Les illustrés pour enfants*. Tourcoing, Duvivier, 1920.

BOOK IV

G. FANCIULLI, E. MONACI. Cf. Chapter I.

M. MESSO, *Le origini e le vicende del* Cuore *di Edmondo de Amicis* (*L'Illustrazione italiana,* October 1, 1922).

JACQUES ZEILLER, *Madame de Ségur et les enfants.* Fribourg (Suisse), Imprimerie de l'œuvre de Saint-Paul, 1911.

M. SULLY, *Madame de Ségur.* Paris, Lethielleux, 1913.

M. POPP, *Julius Verne und sein Werk.* Vienna, Hartleben, 1909.

EMILE HENRIOT, *Sur un imagier* (*Le Temps,* 28 septembre 1931).

BOOK V

PAUL DOTTIN. Cf. Chapter II.

E. TONNELAT, *Les Frères Grimm.* Paris, Colin, 1912.

M. GIBB, *Le roman de Bas de Cuir.* Paris, Champion, 1927.

GÉDÉON HUET, *Les contes populaires.* Paris, Flammarion, 1923.

MANNHARDT, *Wald-und Feldkulte.* Berlin, Borntraeger, 1875-1877, 2 vol.

FLORIS DELATTRE, *Le Peter Pan de J. M. Barrie* (*Revue pédagogique,* 15 décembre 1908).

SCHEID, *L'évolution du sens littéraire chez l'enfant* (*Revue pédagogique,* janvier 1912).

A. M. JORDAN, *Children's Interest in Reading.* The University of Carolina Press, 1926.

E. EVANS, *Trends in Children's Books* (*The New Republic,* November 10, 1926).

G. STREM, *Les contes populaires et les aspirations humaines* (*La Revue mondiale,* 15 mai 1931).

CLAIRE HUCHET, *Les livres pour les enfants* (*La Nouvelle Education,* mars 1927).

M. LABRY-HOLLEBECQUE, *Les charmeurs d'enfants.* Préface de M. Edouard Herriot. Paris, Baudinière, 1927.